AMONG THE 'OTHERS'

Encounters with
the forgotten
Turkmen of Iraq

**By bestselling author and
award-winning journalist**

Scott Taylor

To
Greg with best
wishes
SR

D1264905

ABOUT THE AUTHOR

Scott Taylor, a former soldier, is the editor and publisher of *Esprit de Corps*, an Ottawa-based magazine celebrated for its unflinching scrutiny of the Canadian military. As a war correspondent, Taylor reported from the Persian Gulf during the 1991 *Operation Desert Storm*. He has since made 19 trips into Iraq –before and after Saddam's regime was toppled.

Taylor appears regularly in the Canadian media as a military analyst and is the recipient of the 1996 Quill Award, for outstanding work in the field of Canadian communications. That same year he won the Alexander Mackenzie Award for journalistic excellence.

A columnist for the *Halifax Herald*, the *Windsor Star*, and Osprey newspapers, Taylor has been a contributor to the *Globe and Mail*, *Reader's Digest* and *Media Magazine*. Some of the on-site reporting that appears in this book was produced while on freelance assignments for *the Ottawa Citizen*, *Toronto Sun*, *Maclean's*, *Aljazeera* (English-language news web service), *Dnevnik* (*Macedonian Daily*) and *Magyar Nemzet* (*The Hungarian Nation*).

OTHER WORKS BY SCOTT TAYLOR:

Tarnished Brass: Crime and Corruption in the Canadian Military (co-author with Brian Nolan), 1996 (reprinted paperback 1997)

Tested Mettle: Canada's Peacekeepers at War (co-author with Brian Nolan), 1998

Inat: Images of Serbia and the Kosovo Conflict (author), 2000

Canada at War and Peace, II: A Millennium of Military Heritage (editor-in-chief), 2001

Diary of an Uncivil War: The Violent Aftermath of the Kosovo Conflict (author), 2002

Spinning on the Axis of Evil: America's War Against Iraq (author), 2003

AMONG THE 'OTHERS'

Encounters with the forgotten Turkmen of Iraq

By
Scott Taylor

"The war in Iraq is a rare opportunity to move forward toward an historic period of co-operation. Out of these troubled times ... a new world order can emerge."

George W. Bush, U.S. President, 2003

Printed in Canada

LIBRARY AND ARCHIVES CANADA CATALOGUING IN PUBLICATION
Taylor, Scott, 1960-
Among the others: encounters with the forgotten Turkmen of
Iraq / ScottTaylor

Includes index.
ISBN 1-895896-26-6

1.Turkmen-- Iraq--History 2.Turkmen--Iraq. I. Title
DS70.8.T85T39 2004   956.7'0049'4364   C2004-905247-0

Printed and bound in Canada

Esprit de Corps Books
#204 - 1066 Somerset Street West, Ottawa, Ontario, Canada K1Y 4T3
Tel: (613) 725-5060 /   Fax: (613) 725-1019
e-mail: espritdecorp@idirect.com
www.espritdecorps.ca

ACKNOWLEDGEMENTS

I wish to acknowledge the contribution of the following individuals whose assistance made this project possible. Instrumental in bringing this book to fruition was Asif Sertturkmen who first facilitated the essential support and necessary access from the Iraqi Turkmen Front (ITF). In Ankara, Ahmet Muratli and the staff at the ITF office were always enthusiastic in supporting my ventures into Iraq, and their courtesy is to be commended.

The publisher wishes to acknowledge the contribution of Hasan Ozmen and the Turkmeneli Foundation.

For providing me with background information and research material, Dr. Mustafa Ziya, Zeynep Tugrul and Yuksel Aga are all deserving of thanks.

Operational support inside Iraq was tirelessly provided by Anmar Saadi and the numerous border crossings into Iraqi Kurdistan would not have been possible without the aid of Muaffaq Hacioglu.

For their assistance in publishing my original field reports, credit is due to my editors: Bruce Garvey (*Ottawa Citizen*), Terry O'Neill (*Halifax Herald*), Mike Burke Gaffrey (*Toronto Sun*), Nabil Haji (*Aljazeera*) and Global TV producer George Browne.

The final edit by Bill Twatio and Julie Simoneau really helped to pull this work together, and production assistants Donna Tillotson and Diana Rank also merit praise.

A special thanks is also due to Mary, Raymond and the Kirkness family for their continued support of *Esprit de Corps*.

For Katherine and Kirk Taylor, words alone cannot convey my gratitude for their patience and understanding in allowing me to pursue these ventures. Thanks.

Dedicated to the long-suffering Turkmen of Iraq and their proud struggle to preserve their cultural identity in the face of political oppression and ethnic violence.

ABOUT THIS BOOK

The title is derived from the fact that despite constituting approximately ten per cent of Iraq's population, the "forgotten" Turkmen are often grouped with other factions when foreign analysts and commentators refer to the ethnic makeup of Iraq. In discussions concerning post-war political representation, it is common to hear specific reference made to Shiite Arabs, Sunni Arabs, and Kurds, while the remaining factions—the Turkmen, Yazidi, Sabia, Marsh Arabs, etc.—are often collectively referred to as the "others".

In fact, many people are surprised to learn about the presence of the indigenous Turkmen population—despite the fact that Turkmen settlements were established over fifteen hundred years ago in Iraq. Furthermore, during the past century the Turkmen have been deliberately repressed by successive Iraqi regimes. Under Saddam Hussein's drastic Arabification policy, little official mention was ever made of the distinct Turkmen society of northern Iraq. In addition, Kurdish warlords, who have long coveted control of the oil-rich region of Kirkuk, view any promotion of the Turkmen majority that resides there as a direct threat to their claims.

In addition to presenting a history of the Turkmen people in Iraq, the book also includes several of Scott Taylor's first-hand observations and encounters with Iraqi Turkmen. The book presents a very personal account of a people that have suffered through decades of political oppression and ethnic violence.

SOURCES

While much of this book is drawn from personal experiences, with attributed quotes denoting the source, historical references were drawn largely from:

Paris: 1919, Margaret MacMillan (Random House, 2001)
Challenge to Genocide, Ramsey Clark (IAC Press, 1998)
Iraq at the Crossroads, Toby Dodge and Steven Simon (Oxford University Press, 2003)
Iraq: 30 Years of Progress, Saddam Hussein (1998)

ABOVE: *Map of Iraq identifying some of the cities and places visited by the author on his 19 trips into the region.*

NOTE TO READERS: *The place names on this map—and throughout the book—may differ from other official sources. The English spellings in* Among the 'Others' *are based on phonetic translations of the original Turkish, Arabic or Kurdish names. The same applies to names of individuals.*

ABOVE: *A young vendor peddles cold water to motorists in the city of Kirkuk.* (SCOTT TAYLOR)

OPPOSITE PAGE: *The crusade-era castle dominates the skyline of the ancient Turkmen city of Talafar.* (SCOTT TAYLOR)

Chapter One
"What's a Turkmen?"

NUSAYBIN, TURKEY — It was about mid-morning on April 1, 2003, when the Turkish Jendarma boarded the bus demanding to see every passenger's identification. As the officers worked their way to the back of the bus, they quickly noticed that two of the passengers did not look like the others—on a vehicle jammed with Kurdish farmers, it was impossible to miss two foreign journalists.

Without even asking to see our passports, Sasha Uzunov and I were instructed to grab our luggage and get off the bus. The U.S. intervention in Iraq had begun five days earlier and, like hundreds of other journalists not embedded with coalition forces or already in Baghdad, Sasha and I were trying to gain access into Iraq via the Turkish border.

Officially the Turkish government had closed the border several weeks before the war began. However, despite the fact that Turkey had rejected a request by the United States to allow them access, American troops nevertheless openly used eastern Turkey as a staging area for their pre-war build up in northern Iraq. To keep a lid on this public deception, the Turkish authorities had established several press centres in the border region and, in co-operation with the Jendarma, foreign media were being closely monitored. For instance, any reporter caught photographing U.S. soldiers entering Iraq faced paying an automatic $2,000 US fine and the seizure of all camera equipment.

The fact that Sasha, a stockily-built former Australian soldier-turned-war correspondent, and I were on the bus had caused the Jendarma undue alarm. We had registered ourselves at the Turkish press office in Diyarbakir, and we were authorized to travel the 300 kilometres to the border town of Silopi. This was where some 700 international journalists were waiting for the authorities to reopen the border, or were plotting some way to cross into Iraq illegally. As most of the journalists had hired private cars, the Jendarma were naturally suspicious to find two ex-soldiers on a filthy, overcrowded local bus.

At this highway checkpoint were two squads of Jendarma, consisting of two armoured vehicles parked alongside a bombed-out building. Since 1984, the Kurdish Workers Party (PKK) had waged a 15-year bloody separatist insurgency throughout this area of eastern Turkey. After the deaths of over 30,000 civilians and the displacement of thousands more Kurdish villagers, the Turkish authorities had managed to capture PKK leader Abdullah Ocalan in 1999. With Ocalan in captivity, the remaining PKK fighters had fled into northern Iraq where they signed a shaky ceasefire. However, as the U.S. intervention in Iraq threatened to destabilize the entire region, the Jendarma remained alert to the possibility of a renewed

PKK offensive.

Owing to the volume of radio traffic and standard military bureaucratic procedures, it took several hours for the Jendarma lieutenant to clear our credentials with his superiors. In the meantime, the Turkish conscripts were polite and eager to chat about the war.

"Beneath these uniforms we are still Turks. And like our countrymen, we too are opposed to this war," said the lieutenant, as he handed us back our passports. "How do you think we feel having to do America's dirty work here in our own country?"

Although Sasha and I were now free to continue on our way, we were faced with the problem of transportation. With no one permitted to cross the border, the normally busy highway was practically deserted and the next bus was not due to pass for several hours. Our dilemma was resolved by the timely arrival of a three-man British television crew. The Jendarma lieutenant's request left little room for refusal, and despite the protests of the TV producer we were soon crammed into the back seat of their Audi—along with all of our luggage and an overweight cameraman.

Sasha, irritable after the long delay at the checkpoint, grumbled that our new-found travel companions were a "bunch of soft-cocks"—a phrase he used to describe anyone from England or anybody less macho than Chuck Norris—before promptly falling asleep.

Although none of the Brits had ever been to Iraq before, it didn't stop them from speaking authoritatively on the subject. As they began discussing which of the two Iraqi Kurdish warlords was most likely to gain post-war control of the oil fields around Kirkuk, I could not help but ask, "What about the Turkmen?" The fact that I had dared to speak drew a condescending scowl from the producer, but the reporter seemed intrigued.

"What's a Turkmen?" he asked.

Giving them the *Reader's Digest* version, I quickly explained that there were about 2 million ethnic Turkmen living in northern Iraq. Descendants of ancient Turkish tribes, these indigenous Iraqis constitute almost 10 per cent of the population and, after the Arabs and Kurds, formed the third largest ethnic group. More importantly, they constitute the majority of Kirkuk's population, which has long been considered a Turkmen city.

"Can you prove any of what you are telling me?" asked the reporter. Having only the day before interviewed Dr. Mustafa Ziya, at the time director of the Iraqi Turkmen Front in Ankara, I happened to have volumes of documentation on hand. After rooting around in my briefcase to produce a handful of books, pamphlets and even maps illustrating the Turkmenli zone of Iraq, the reporter asked in a conspiratorial tone, "Will you share this with me?"

I hardly considered the presence of an ethnic faction in Iraq to be my personal domain, so I willingly agreed. Almost immediately, he used a satellite phone to call his desk in London. As all the field correspondents at this stage of the war were begging their producers for "face-time", he apparently thought this information would give him an edge. "I need a full 10 minutes on the Saturday show," he said. "Why? Because there has been a whole new development in northern Iraq."

Like Christopher Columbus's "discovery" of North America, already populated by aboriginal people, the 1500-year-old existence of the Turkmen in Iraq became "news" when foreign reporters first learned of them. The British background piece on the Turkmen never did make it onto the air as a friendly fire incident in northern Iraq, which killed a number of Kurdish peshmerga militia men, had much more dramatic footage.

The Turkmen would remain "forgotten"—at least on British television.

ADMITTEDLY, IT HAD TAKEN me several trips to fully discover the country's vast ethnic and cultural diversity, and it was not until my eighth trip to Baghdad that I happened to stumble onto the existence of the Turkmen.

My original purpose in heading into Iraq was to report on the 10-year aftermath of the first Gulf War. Having spent the spring of 1999 in Serbia and Kosovo during the NATO bombardment, I had long since realized that there is always an "other side" to war reports and that U.S. and NATO allies were certainly capable of fabricating justifications for their military actions.

I knew that the economic embargo imposed by the United Nations in August 1990 was still in place against Saddam Hussein's regime, but I had not realized that U.S. and British air strikes in Iraq had continued almost constantly since the so-called ceasefire was brokered after the liberation of Kuwait in 1991. Unreported by Western journalists, America had been waging a secret war of containment and punishment against Iraq for over a decade. In August 2000, I happened to be the only foreign reporter in Iraq and, as such, I was the sole independent witness to a U.S. air strike in the southern city of Samawa. I spent an afternoon interviewing the civilian casualties and photographing the destruction. To authenticate my research I even climbed down inside one of the craters to re-trieve a piece of an American missile.

Two Iraqis had been killed and another 19 seriously injured. The destroyed buildings included a United Nations food dis-tribution centre and the local train station. The Pentagon's claim that U.S. aircraft had fired in self-defence and destroyed Iraqi air defence weapons was simply not supported by the evidence. However, when my story was published in the *Ottawa Citizen*, the Pentagon responded by releasing an undated satellite photo of destroyed anti-aircraft cannons to "prove" their point. Those in the Washington press corps that even bothered to notice the story bought the fabrication and my eyewitness account was dismissed as "inaccurate."

It was during my first trip into Iraq that I made the ac-quaintance of Jabar Abu Marwan, who was assigned to be my guide. Although he was officially working for the Foreign Min-istry, the slightly-built, but obviously very fit Jabar made it clear from the outset that he was an agent in the Mukhabarat, Iraqi's secret service. As a member of the North American branch, Jabar had spent a couple of years at the Iraqi embassy in Ottawa. We had mutual friends in the Iraqi-Canadian com-munity, are the same age and, although a Shiite Muslim, Jabar had frequented many of the same pubs I did in Canada's capi-tal. Over a bottle of Scotch in my hotel room, we soon became friends, and Jabar proved to be an invaluable source of infor-mation in addition to being my guide.

At that time, Saddam's regime was desperate to end the crippling UN embargo, and for any foreign journalist that did manage to enter Iraq, there were certain must-see-must-tell items of interest. While it was virtually impossible to meet with senior ministers or officials, the Iraqi Foreign Ministry made every effort to get journalists to visit the hospitals. The children's wards were the most disturbing. Following the massive bombardments of the first Gulf War, not only were the water and sewage treatment plants destroyed, but entire regions were contaminated with radioactive residue from U.S. and British depleted uranium munitions.

After the war, water borne diseases like diphtheria, typhoid and dysentery killed nearly 1.2 million Iraqis, and the effects of exposed to depleted uranium (DU) had generated an epidemic of leukemia in children and a rash of inexplicable birth defects. To visit those wards and photograph the children was emotionally one of the toughest assignments I have ever had.

Under the harsh restrictions of the UN sanctions, Iraq could not acquire anything that was considered nuclear dual-use technology. As a result, radiation and chemotherapy treatments which could have saved as many as 70 per cent of leukemia cases were not available. Children simply waited to die.

Incredibly, this did not seem to unduly concern U.S. authorities. In late 1995, when asked on the U.S. news program *60 Minutes* whether the U.S. policy toward Iraq could possibly justify the deaths of 500,000 children, then Secretary of State Madeleine Albright didn't hesitate: "Yes, the price is worth it." Ms. Albright may have had a different opinion if she had spent an afternoon in Baghdad's Saddam Central Teaching Hospital for Children, observing the grim results of that policy.

While the Iraqi authorities certainly wanted to demonstrate to me the impact of the UN-imposed embargo on civilians, they were less than pleased when I wrote an article describing the deplorable state of Saddam's once impressive military. Everywhere I travelled, I had been able to observe Iraqi soldiers—from the conscripted, poorly trained reserve air defence gunners stationed in Baghdad to the supposedly elite Republican Guard airborne divisions deployed around Basra. The Iraqi army obviously had become a shadow of its former self.

Standard issue boots seemed to be in short supply as many of the soldiers wore sandals. Their Kalashnikov assault rifles were so old that the wooden stocks were scarred and the metallic bluing on the breeches had long since worn off. In many of the tank depots, where rows of armoured vehicles had once been parked in the shade, only flocks of sheep could be seen. In the vicinity of Basra, on the "Highway of Death" from Kuwait I had seen the vast piles of destroyed tanks and armoured personnel carriers that had been reduced to scrap by the U.S. Air Force in 1991 during the Iraqi army's desperate retreat.

In military outposts where armoured vehicles were placed defiantly atop the sand berm protective walls, birds nested inside the road wheels. With no spare parts or replacement vehicles, the Iraqi army had curtailed most of its training exercises to conserve its few remaining resources. Instead of real armoured vehicles, army units were usually seen patrolling in Nissan and Toyota pickup trucks with a machine gun mounted on the cab.

Although Saddam's military still possessed an abundance of air defence weaponry, most of it was antiquated low-level cannon and machine guns. Whatever rockets and radar the Iraqis still had, they had long since proven useless against the technologically superior allied air forces that regularly pummelled targets inside Iraq with complete impunity. British intelligence reported that between 1991 and 2000, Iraq had fired over 7,000 rockets at allied aircraft patrolling the no-fly zones without downing a single plane. For its part, the Iraqi air force remained largely quarantined in Iran where it had been flown for safekeeping at the outset of the first Gulf War. The few helicopters that remained in service could only operate safely in the central region of Iraq, which was not included in the U.S. imposed no-fly zones in the north and south.

After my story on the Iraqi military was published, Jabar Abu Marwan advised me that the generals were not pleased. "Although what you wrote is true, they are offended to see their troops described in such a manner," he said. "It will be difficult for you to get another entry visa, but be patient; they will soon forget about this."

Besides the worn-out state of the military, Jabar explained to me that another very touchy subject in senior circles was the 1991 post-Gulf War uprisings that had nearly toppled Saddam. When his shattered divisions fled north from Kuwait, Shiite fundamentalists took advantage of the chaos to overthrow local Baath party officials. While in the north, Kurdish warlords launched their private peshmerga militias into central Iraq, hoping to gain control of Kirkuk's oilfields. In Baghdad, the impoverished Shiite residents of the slum known as Saddam City (now Sadr City) took the opportunity to overwhelm police and security forces and go on a wild looting spree.

"Americans always talk about the atrocities committed by Saddam's loyalist troops when they suppressed the uprising," said Jabar. "The U.S. never acknowledges the bloody violence which they themselves initiated by encouraging the insurgents." The scenes in Basra and Kerbala had been some of the most horrific: with crowds of cheering onlookers watched as Saddam's officials and top military officers were tied between two car bumpers and then literally torn in half as the vehicles accelerated in opposite directions.

"In the summer of 1991, Saddam only had control of three provinces; twelve were in open revolt and three remained under Kurdish control," said Jabar "By November, after much heavy fighting the rebellion was suppressed." However, as part of the UN-brokered ceasefires, the three northernmost provinces of Iraq remained under the autonomous control of Kurdish warlords. Massoud Barzani's Kurdistan Democratic Party (KDP) held Dohuk and Erbil, while rival Jalal Talabani's Patriotic Union of Kurdistan (PUK) controlled the northeastern region of Sulaimaniyah.

Although the oil riches of Kirkuk remained inside Saddam's zone of influence, under the strictly monitored UN oil-for-food program, the Kurd-controlled region also received a percentage of Iraq's oil export revenue. During the post-war period, the complexities of northern Iraqi politics had resulted in a number of armed clashes between the KDP and PUK. The most serious confrontation occurred in 1996 when Massoud Barzani brokered a deal with Saddam Hussein. In a whirlwind military offensive supported by Iraqi armour pushing north, Barzani's KDP scored a major victory over the PUK.

As part of the bargain, Saddam's Mukhabarat agents were given a free hand to eliminate the entire Central Intelligence Agency operation in Iraqi Kurdistan. The U.S. intelligence agents had eagerly set up shop in the Kurdish zone following the ceasefire in 1991, and had used these bases to infiltrate into Saddam's provinces. Although the 1996 clashes took place inside the northern no-fly zone, the U.S. and British air forces could not fly intervention sorties because their mandate did not include a Kurd-versus-Kurd scenario. In the wake of these clashes, the U.S., Britain and Turkey established the Peace Monitoring Force in northern Iraq. It was a complex under-

TOP: *Iraqi soldiers surrendering during 1991 Operation Desert Storm. (RICHARD KEMP)* **CENTRE:** *Some of the nearly 200,000 Iraqi casualties from the first Gulf War—one of the most one-sided military encouters of all time.(RICHARD KEMP)* **ABOVE LEFT:** *The scene of destruction outside Kuwait City in the aftermath of Iraq's defeat.* **ABOVE RIGHT:** *Hans Blix, chief weapons inspector for the United Nations. (UN PHOTO BY ESKINDER DEBEBE)*

TOP: A Kurdish casualty of the 1988 chemical weapon attack in Halabja. (IRAN PHOTO FOUNDATION) **ABOVE:** Canadian soldier with 1CER examines the carnage on the Highway of Death. (SCOTT TAYLOR) **RIGHT:** Kurdish peshmerga staged a brief rebellion against Saddam Hussein's regime in 1991. (AP)

taking whereby Special Forces troops from these three countries provided training to the Kurdish peshmerga.

Jabar explained that a third Kurdish faction – the Ansar al-Islam Shiite fundamentalists – also factored into this equation. Sponsored by Iran, this organization had wreaked havoc in northern Iraq during the Iran-Iraq War in the 1980s. In March 1988, Saddam had aligned himself with Talabani's PUK to eliminate Ansar al-Islam's stronghold in Halabja. It was during this joint Kurdish-Iraqi operation that chemical weapons were deployed, resulting in an estimated 5,000 civilian casualties.

"The U.S. propaganda machine always refers to the Halabja massacre as 'Saddam gassing his own people,' but they never mention that America provided the chemicals and Kurds helped in the operation," said Jabar hastily adding, "but no one can justify the killing of innocent civilians. That was a regrettable tragedy."

Although he was able to give me detailed accounts of the situation with the various Kurdish warlords, Jabar never once spoke to me about the Turkmen. I later concluded that this must have been in part due to Jabar's belief in Saddam's policy of Arabification. Unlike the Kurds who exercised a fair degree of autonomy, particularly after 1991 when they were granted self-rule, the Turkmen were taught Arabic in schools and listed as Arabs on most official documents. Despite the ethnic and religious divisions in the country, Saddam maintained a policy of pan-Arabism and portrayed himself as the only Arab leader willing to stand up to the "Israeli Zionists and their American puppets." It did not fit the Baath party agenda to acknowledge either Kurdish or Turkmen claims to Kirkuk's oil reserves, which constitutes some 40 per cent of Iraq's total supply.

It was not until October 2002, when U.S. President George W. Bush began beating the war drums that I first became aware of the Iraqi Turkmen. The occasion was Saddam Hussein's presidential referendum. Billed as a "demonstration of honest democracy," the Iraqi people were allowed to cast their votes for the only candidate on the ballot – Saddam Hussein. I was part of a group of nearly 1,000 foreign media and international observers that were on hand in Baghdad to witness "the people's love for Saddam."

At a pre-election press conference, Iraq's Minister of Information, Mohammed Saeed Al-Sahaf – who would go on to wartime fame as "Comical Ali" – made the first of many classic denials to the assembled foreign media, categorically denying that this eleventh hour leadership vote was being staged to undermine Bush's calls for a "regime change in Iraq."

"We do not submit to outside pressures – that would be stupid," said Al-Sahaf. "The people of Iraq will send their message of support for Saddam whether or not there is a threat of war. Whether this will be accepted in the West is irrelevant." However, when asked to explain why the majority of the election banners were written in English and displayed in front of hotels housing foreigners, Minister Al-Sahaf refused to answer. Prophetically, the Minister of Information then announced, "There is no need for estimations. You will see positive results." With the local Mukhabarat conducting the election, the prediction that Saddam would win 100 per cent of the vote seemed a given.

The Turkish journalists in the crowded conference hall began asking Al-Sahaf for specific information about Turkmen voters. The documentation provided to the media indicated that there were a total of 11,798,000 eligible voters registered in the 15 provinces still under Saddam's rule, but there was no specific breakdown based on ethnicity. As nearly half of Iraq's Turkmen population lives in the three Kurd-controlled provinces in the north, Al-Sahaf assured the Turkish reporter that any Turkmen living above the administrative Kurdish boundary who wished to make the trip to show their love for Saddam by voting would be welcomed to do so. Al-Sahaf conceded that the Turkish delegation could travel by bus to Kirkuk to observe the referendum results if they wished.

My curiosity peaked by the questions raised by the Turkish journalists, I asked one of them why they were heading to Kirkuk. "Because that is where the Turkmen live," she replied.

It was my turn to ask: "What's a Turkmen?"

ABOVE: *Massive demonstrations were organized across Iraq to show support for Saddam Hussein prior to the October 2002 election. (JASSIM MOHAMMED/AP)*

ABOVE: *Crusaders had a difficult time fighting through Asia Minor. Turkmen mercenaries in the Muslim armies helped to keep the Christian soldiers out of modern-day Iraq. (BBC HULTON PICTURE LIBRARY)*
OPPOSITE PAGE: *Turkish troops shown advancing into Persia.*

Chapter Two
Deep Roots

ONE OF THE MOST DIFFICULT and contentious issues surrounding the Iraqi Turkmen is trying to figure out exactly how many of them exist. Everyone you ask will provide a different answer, with numbers ranging as high as 4 million according to Iraqi Turkmen nationalists, to as little as the 136,800 claimed by Kurdish authorities. In a small, modern third-floor office in downtown Ankara, Dr. Habib Hurmuzlo, the director of Global Strategy Institute, a Middle East think tank, explained to me the reasons for this vast discrepancy in numbers.

"There were two national census results, one released in 1957, with a corrected number released after the revolution in 1958. As there has not been any effort to record ethnic divisions since that date," explained Dr. Hurmuzlo, "all statistics are based on these original census results."

Born in 1933 in the city of Kirkuk, Dr. Hurmuzlo spent most of his life studying the origins of Turkish culture, and is con-

sidered an expert when it comes to defining the Iraqi Turkmen. According to the 1957 census conducted by King Faisal
II—a monarch supported by the British—there were only
136,800 Turkmen in all of Iraq. Bearing in mind that since the
British had wrested control of Mesopotamia from the Turks
after the First World War, a deliberate campaign had been undertaken to eradicate or diminish all remnants of Ottoman
influence. Therefore, it should not be surprising that after
Abdul Karim Kassem launched his successful revolution in
1958—killing 23-year-old King Faisal II, expelling the British
and declaring Iraq a republic – that a different set of numbers
was published. According to the second census of 1958, the
Turkmen registry stood at 567,000—an increase of more than
400 per cent from the previous year's total.

At that time, the entire population of Iraq was just 7 million. So while it is not scientifically accurate, if the Turkmen
simply kept pace with the rest of Iraq's birthrate, then they
would now account for approximately 2,080,000 of the present
day 25 million inhabitants. Many Turkmen argue that their
birthrate actually exceeds that of most of the other Iraqi ethnic
groups. One need only visit the children-filled streets of Talafar to believe their claim. However, for the sake of argument,
a general figure of 2 million should be used until a new census
is conducted. For their purposes, the Kurds have stuck to the
original 1957 figure of 136,800 without allowing for any population growth whatsoever over the past five decades.

In September 2003, Laci Zoldi, a Hungarian colleague, had
arranged to accompany me during a post-war visit to report
on the continuing violence in Iraq. At the time, it was still difficult to cross the Iraq-Turkey border, but my contacts in the
Iraqi Turkmen Front (ITF) had made arrangements for our safe

passage. Laci had visited Baghdad before—in fact, this is where I first met him—but he had never been to the northern provinces. Likeable and outgoing, Laci was a dead the ringer for a young Donny Osmond. He had been able to transcend cultural barriers easily and quickly made friends with many Iraqis during and after his inaugural trip to Baghdad. However, the Iraqi expatriate contacts that Laci had established in Budapest were all of Kurdish descent. When he had told them about his impending travel plans, arranged by the Iraqi Turkmen Front, they had been quick to produce the unadjusted 1957 census documents to "prove" that the Turkmen were nothing more than a marginal minority.

However, even if one was to factor in the proportional increase based on the flawed 1957 census (which the CIA does), this would only amount to 490,000 Turkmen. The fact that this number alone is found in the Turkmen enclave of Talafar seriously undermines those calculations. In the region defined loosely as Turkmenli, there are 12 major cities and towns containing sizeable concentrations of Turkmen—not the least of which is the ancestral heartland of Kirkuk.

One of the difficulties in trying to chart the historical links of any one people such as the Turkmen in modern day Iraq is that the artificially created nation occupies the territory described as the "Cradle of Civilization." For almost 6,000 years the land between the Tigris and Euphrates rivers has been a magnet for invasion and the birthplace of many great empires. Each successive military occupation brought cultural and ethnic changes, as did the expansion of Assyrian and Babylonian dynasties. While all of present-day Iraq's rulers used an iron fist to keep a lid on internal dissent, it has nevertheless always been necessary for them to form strategic alliances within this multi-ethnic society.

Determining how far back the Turkmen presence in Iraq dates is often the subject of heated debate, even among Turkmen historians. Part of the problem lies in the fact that the ancient Oguz Turkic tribes of central Asia made more than one westward migration, from the region of present-day Turkmenistan and Uzbekistan. The Oguz people were eventually forced out completely by the Kirghiz, another Turkic tribe, and scattered throughout Asia Minor, including northern Iraq.

The loose definition of the term Oguz (meaning tribes) suggests that these were not a homogeneous people but rather a closely-knit union of different tribes, all speaking related, but not identical dialects. Those Oguz who converted to Islam became known as Turkmen, and numerous clashes erupted between them and non-Muslim Oguz tribes. Having honed their fighting skills and earned a reputation as disciplined warriors, Turkmen soldiers, particularly archers, were recruited into the Muslim armies of Ubaydullah Bin Ziyad in the mid-7th century. The first recorded presence of Turkmen in Iraq dates back to 650 AD, when Bin Ziyad deployed about 2,000 warriors in the vicinity of Basra in southern Iraq.

During the subsequent Abbassid era, thousands more Turkmen warriors were brought into Iraq from Turkmenistan to fight as mercenaries. Although many of the soldiers and their camp followers settled in their new homeland, their numbers were not significant. As a result, it is widely believed that this "first wave" of Turkmen became assimilated into the local Arab population over the passage of time.

The second wave of Turkmen to descend on Iraq was to have a far more lasting presence. Again, it came in the form of

Oguz warriors, this time serving in the Seljuk army under the command of Sultan Tugrul Bey. In 1055, under the pretext that he intended to repair the holy road to Mecca, Sultan Bey assembled an army and marched on Baghdad. For the next 150 years, the Turkmen continued to move into what is now northern Iraq where they established a permanent presence. During the Crusades, the Turkmen once again played a leading role in the Muslim armies, and the Christian soldiers were unable to penetrate beyond the western fringes of modern day Iraq.

Warfare and conquest brought a third wave of Oguz soldiers into the region during the Ottoman Empire. The largest number of Turkmen immigrants followed the army of Sultan Suleiman the Magnificent when he conquered all of Iraq in 1535. Throughout their reign, the Ottomans encouraged the settlement of immigrant Turkmen along the loosely formed boundary that divided Arab and Kurdish settlements in northern Iraq. With loyal Turkmen inhabiting this area, the Ottoman armies were able to secure their supply lines and maintain a safe route through to the southern provinces of Mesopotamia.

As Ottoman rule in Iraq did not end until 1919, following Turkey's defeat in the First World War, there is often a false perception that the Turkmen of Iraq are recent "trespassers"— a remnant from a conquering empire. To put this in perspective, even if one were to discount the first migratory settlements as "insignificant" and date the Turkmen presence in Iraq beginning in 1535—this still predates the American Declaration of Independence by 241 years.

A visit to the Turkmen city of Talafar, in the governate of Dohuk, is like stepping back in time to the Middle Ages. From the stone embrasures of the Crusade-era fortress, to the goatherds grazing their flocks in the deep ravines, everything about this remote city in western Iraq indicates ancient history. "Most of the residents here are living in houses that are older than America," said Dr. Yashar Talafarli, a tall and distinguished-looking 46-year-old father of four and the local Turkmen community leader in Talafar. "How can anyone suggest that after more than 400 years of inhabiting this region we don't belong here? What would they say about the Europeans who have inhabited North America over roughly the same time frame?"

It is also impossible to group the Iraqi Turkmen under a single religious affiliation. Although the majority are Sunni Muslims, there are a larger number of Shiite Turkmen, some Islamic fundamentalists, and even a group of Chaldean Christians in the mix. "The Chaldean Turkmen priests lived for centuries in the castle at Kirkuk," explained Dr. Yashar. "That was until Saddam Hussein mounted his Arabification policy and they were expelled."

However, as the very existence of the Iraqi Turkmen Front —a collection of 19 different political parties and organizations and religious groups—indicates, these people identify themselves first and foremost by their Turkmen roots. "For instance, a Shiite Turkmen would not align himself with a Shiite Arab against a Sunni Turkmen brother," said Dr. Yashar. "And because of our collective minority status, we have no serious divisions among our own people." Historically, considerable enmity has existed between the Turkmen and the Kurds, particularly in the past century, although the encroachment of Kurdish influence in northern Iraq began when the Turkish sultans ruled the area.

The pre-1919 association between the Iraqi Turkmen and the displaced Ottomans is something which is often misunderstood. While one would expect Turkish officials to give preferential treatment to those Iraqis who share their language and culture, this was not always the case. Born in the city of Erbil in 1924, just five years after the Turks were expelled, Adil Taha Muratli has vivid childhood memories of his father's description of the Ottoman Empire.

"He worked for the government as a junior civil servant, but he often complained that the Turks would give the best jobs and promotions to the Arabs and Kurds as a means of keeping the peace and in an attempt to buy their loyalty," recalled the elderly Muratli. "In fact, it seems hard to believe but in many ways things actually improved for us when the British Army came into Iraq."

LEFT: Contemporary portrait of Sultan Suleiman the Magnificent. By 1535, the Sultan had conquered all of modern-day Iraq. It was during this period that the main migration of ethnic Turkmen entered into Iraq. Throughout four centuries of subsequent Ottoman rule, the Turkmen settlements in northern Iraq provided a safe supply and communication route into southern Iraq for the Turkish garrisons.

ABOVE: British troops march triumphantly northwards in their conquest of Mesopotamia. (IMPERIAL WAR MUSEUM)
OPPOSITE PAGE: King Faisal I and T.E. Lawrence (of Arabia), pictured at right of the King, were disappointed with the post-war division of the Middle East during the 1919 Paris peace talks. (IMPERIAL WAR MUSEUM)

Chapter Three
After the Ottomans

FEBRUARY 2003, KIRKUK, IRAQ — With George W. Bush's threats to remove Saddam Hussein mounting and war seeming imminent, Iraq had become a monthly whistle-stop on my reporting schedule. Whereas on my previous visits only a handful of Western journalists had been in Baghdad, now hundreds of international reporters were settling themselves in the Iraqi capital in anticipation of the expected conflict. The Mukhabarat agents assigned to monitor foreigners were overwhelmed. In an effort to control this newly arrived horde, the Mukhabarat and the Iraqi Ministry of Information placed tight restrictions on all internal travel and media access. Saddam Hussein had declared publicly that he would turn Baghdad into an "impenetrable fortress." As a result, even taking photographs of public areas—including historical landmarks—was suddenly forbidden.

With so many journalists being simply herded back and

forth between their hotels and official Iraqi government press conferences, I had decided that a trip outside of Baghdad would provide me with a different perspective. In particular, I had asked permission from my Mukhabarat contacts to cross the administrative boundary and visit the Kurd-controlled provinces of northern Iraq. As part of the official spin I had been repeatedly told, I was supposed to believe that Saddam and the Kurdish warlords were one big, happy family—despite the recent wars. I didn't accept this of course, and I was anxious to call their bluff. During previous visits to Iraq I had twice ventured north to the city of Mosul, and with a Ministry of Information handler in tow, I had even spent a day visiting Iraqi soldiers stationed along the Kurdish boundary.

However, with the Mukhabarat running around day and night trying to keep tabs on all their new foreign charges, my official request to travel north had obviously been buried in a mountain of paperwork. Unable to make direct contact with my usual Mukhabarat guides, I decided to bend the rules a little. While I had no formal authorization to travel outside of Baghdad on this trip, I had earlier assurances that this would be admissible. So, in the absence of any official sanction, I struck a deal with my driver, Anmar Saadi.

Over several drinks one night, we had discussed the possibility of driving north out of Baghdad to Kirkuk, and then trying to bluff our way past the border guards. It was admittedly a ridiculous scheme given all the pre-war controls in Saddam's Iraq, but Anmar figured that if we acted with enough authority at the highway checkpoints, the guards would be too frightened of a superior's wrath to challenge us. Having been a member of Saddam's Presidential Guard, Anmar was a veteran soldier and he well understood the fear-driven mentality of his former comrades. Although I knew the Mukhabarat would be furious with me for running around the country on my own, I figured that, by the time I got back, it would be too late for them to do anything and I would beg their forgiveness.

Heavily fortified with 'liquid courage,' we left Baghdad after dark the following evening. Anmar owned a battered old Volkswagen Passat, and we felt that if our bluff was to work darkness would be an asset. It was Anmar's intention to challenge the Iraqi police at each successive roadblock. By stating authoritatively that this was an official delegation, and then asking them for some simple directions such as "Is this road to Kirkuk?" he hoped they would be caught off guard and unwilling to press us for an explanation as to our travel authority. To our complete incredulity, this trick worked every time and not one of the policemen had the presence of mind to ask us why an official foreign delegate would be driving around in the middle of the night in a beat up old Passat.

The one mistake we made was bringing liquor with us in the car. Anmar's eyesight is not good at the best of times, and as he continued to drink Arrack, he was soon blind drunk. Although his slurred Arabic and erratic driving did not hamper our passage through the police checkpoints, it did slow our trip north to a 40-kilometre-an-hour crawl. With the highway virtually deserted, the 340-kilometre stretch from Baghdad to Kirkuk should not have taken us much more than three hours. However, we were already into our sixth hour of driving when I spotted a fierce orange glow on the horizon.

Given the scale of the blazing fires, I assumed that some major catastrophe had taken place. Anmar, by contrast, was visibly relieved at the sight. "We are almost [in Kirkuk] now.

Those are the gas fires of Baba Gur Gur," he slurred.

As we drove closer, the full extent of this natural phenomenon became apparent. With so much natural gas burning off, creating a veritable fireball on earth, one could only imagine the vastness of the oil deposits buried beneath the ground. This same thought must have crossed the minds of the soldiers with the British Expeditionary Force in Mesopotamia who would have first glimpsed the oil fires in 1918.

~~~~~~~~~~

Until the turn of the 20th century, coal had fuelled the Industrial Revolution. But in the subsequent two decades, oil increasingly gained prominence as a vital resource in the modern world. The transition from coal to oil was further accelerated by the innovations and demands necessitated by the First World War. In fact, Lord George Curzon, a British politician, went so far as to claim that the Allies had swept to victory upon a wave of oil.

In 1914, at the war's outset, Britain's most significant source of oil came from its petroleum holdings in Iran. Ironically, the oil riches in the neighbouring Turk-controlled Mesopotamia had remained undiscovered. It was in an effort to secure Iranian oil that Britain and its commonwealth allies first mounted military attacks against the Turks around the city of Basra. Despite some initial setbacks, the British regrouped and steadily forced the Turkish army northwards. At the time of the armistice in October 1918, the British had occupied two provinces of Basra and Baghdad.

The Turks under the generalship of Ali Ihsan Pasha had successfully prevented the British from penetrating into the

Mosul district, which included the cities of Kirkuk, Sulaimaniyah, Erbil and Dohuk. Under the terms of the October 31, 1918 Mudros Agreement, the Turks were to retain control of this area. However, with the collapse of the Ottoman dynasty and the internal instability surrounding the emergence of Kemal Attaturk and his 'Young Turk' reformers, the British had seized the opportunity to violate the Treaty and push north. Attaturk had reluctantly ordered Pasha's troops to withdraw without a fight. Meanwhile, on the diplomatic front, the president of Turkey demanded that the British conduct a referendum among the residents of the Mosul province to determine whether they preferred British or Turkish rule. With their troops already on the ground, the British simply ignored Attaturk's request. Although by 1919 scientific surveys had yet to be conducted, an initial assessment by the British concluded that, from the oil bubbling out of the ground around Basra and the natural gas fires of Baba Gur Gur, that Mesopotamian petroleum assets were probably "the greatest in the world."

It was this discovery that led the British to reconsider their post-war designs on the region. It had been their original intention to dismantle the crumbling Ottoman Empire, but not to add new territory to their own still extensive list of colonies. As long as Mesopotamia was considered to be a virtually worthless tract of desert, the British had been quite prepared to hand over its control to their wartime Arab allies.

Organized and led by the legendary T.E. Lawrence (of Arabia), Arab guerrillas had mounted a spirited campaign against the Turkish supply routes and rear-area garrisons. The most prominent of the Arab tribal leaders was Faisal, the son of Sherif Hussein. In exchange for his military support, Lawrence assured him that he would be rewarded with own post-war Arab kingdom stretching from Syria into Palestine and Mesopotamia. While the British and French had alienated the Arab world with their 1917 Balfour Declaration, which supported the creation of a Jewish homeland in Palestine, their betrayal of Faisal at the Treaty of Sèvres in 1919 would soon set the Middle East ablaze.

Lawrence had travelled with Faisal to Paris and London to participate in the post-war settlements. However, by September 1919 it had become clear that France intended to keep Syria as a strategic colony and that Britain had no intention of ceding control of its new-found oil wealth in Mesopotamia. Realizing that he had been cut out of the spoils, Faisal returned to Damascus where he devoted himself to the growing Arab independence movement.

Although French troops were still stationed in the newly claimed colony, the Syrian Congress defiantly pronounced Faisal the King of Syria on March 7, 1920. Shortly thereafter a second congress was convened in Damascus and Faisal's brother, Abdullah, was proclaimed ruler of Mesopotamia. King Abdullah's first decree was to denounce the British occupation of his territory, ordering an immediate withdrawal of all foreign troops from Mesopotamia. The French army had moved quickly to crush Faisal's challenge to their colonial authority, and their troops had easily put down the Arab rebellion in Syria. The British chose to simply ignore King Abdullah's ultimatum, and Mesopotamia soon erupted into a series of small guerrilla attacks. In scenes of violence all too reminiscent to those encountered by the U.S.-led coalition forces since their military intervention in Iraq in 2003, Arab resistance fighters attacked railway lines, destroyed telegraph poles, murdered British soldiers and besieged small garrisons across the country.

However, it was not only the Arabs of Mesopotamia that resisted occupation. In the north, Kurdish warlords had been relieved to see the Ottoman Turks withdraw from their territory, only to be alarmed when they were replaced by British-led troops. They recognized that if all three Mesopotamian provinces were to be grouped under one central authority in Baghdad then they would once again be denied a chance for an independent state.

In response to the mounting guerrilla attacks, the British launched punitive air strikes against villages that were suspected of supporting insurgents. At that time, the use of air power to police colonies was an untested tactic, and the architect of this strategy was none other than Arthur Harris. As an air marshal in World War Two he would earn himself the nickname Bomber Harris, but as a young officer he cut his teeth flying sorties against primitive Kurdish villages in northern Mesopotamia. The air strikes proved to be of limited value since the lumbering British biplanes first warned the targeted villagers by broadcasting messages through loudspeakers and dropping leaflets. By the time the bombs were dropped, most villages had long since been evacuated. While this tactic certainly reduced the loss of innocent civilian lives, the destruction of property did little to win over the hearts and minds of those attacked.

Frustrated at the air force's inability to bring the fractious tribes into line, Sir Winston Churchill, the British Colonial Secretary actually advocated that poison gas be dropped onto rebellious Kurdish villages. Despite such drastic tactics, the British military could not suppress the widespread rebellion.

It was during this immediate post-war period of violence and unrest that the Iraqi Turkmen suffered a series of reciprocal attacks at the hands of displaced Armenians. Throughout the latter stages of World War One, the Ottoman Turks had waged a bloody military campaign against Armenian rebels in the eastern provinces of their crumbling empire. Adopting a scorched-earth strategy against the rebels, the Turks had crushed the Armenians and driven many villagers completely out of the region. A large number of displaced Armenians sought refuge in northern Iraq, and as the Turkish troops withdrew from the area they sought revenge on the poorly armed Turkmen villagers who remained behind. Although these Turkmen had no connection to the Turkish army's offensive in Armenia, the displaced refugees exacted a rough justice with virtual impunity upon the Iraqi kinfolk of the Turks as the British troops had their hands full simply protecting their own outposts.

With mounting casualty lists of Commonwealth troops generating domestic political pressure, a desperate Winston Churchill was forced to make concessions. Establishing what was termed the "Arab façade," the British Colonial Office decided to appoint a 'pliable Arab' as a ruling figurehead in the region. To fill the bill, the British sought out the very same man they had betrayed at the Treaty of Sèvres—the now exiled King Faisal. Although he had originally been promised the Kingdom of Trans-Jordan, the self-proclaimed exiled King of Syria, was now offered control of Mesopotamia by the British.

To convince Faisal to accept the kingdom, he was summoned to visit Mesopotamia, where the British had staged a vote to assure him of his own popular support. In a national referendum, the relatively unknown Faisal received an implausible 96 per cent of the votes.

As a result of this rigged referendum, Faisal was convinced to accept the throne position, and on August 23, 1921, he became King of the territory that would henceforth be called Iraq.

Although he was beholden to the British for having established him in power, King Faisal did not prove to be as pliable as the colonial powers originally had hoped. Between 1921 and 1932, Faisal continued his ultimately successful quest to have this fledgling state declared an independent nation, recognized with member status at the newly formed League of Nations. Although the British had conceded to this, they had done so with the technical caveat that Iraq would remain a protectorate. Despite its newly declared independence, King Faisal's monarchy was still supported by a small British garrison consisting of both ground troops and aircraft deployed to protect their mutual interests—namely, Faisal's regime and the resources of British Petroleum.

Although many Arab nationalists and Kurdish separatists viewed Faisal as a puppet, the Turkmen of Iraq initially liked the new king. Even at 80 years of age, Adil Taha Muratli can still recall King Faisal's 1931 visit to the city of Erbil. "I was seven years old at the time, and I was among a group of Turkmen schoolchildren that had been selected to greet the arrival of the King," Muratli told me through an interpreter. "The location of the reception was at the army officers club, and all of us were decked out in our best school uniforms." Muratli's memory of the King was that he wore a traditional Turkmen *sidare* hat in recognition of the fact that, Erbil's population at the time was predominantly Turkmen. "The cheers from the crowd were genuine, we really loved him."

Politically, the relationship between the Turkmen and the British-supported Faisal monarchy was a little more tenuous. One prominent Turkmen was appointed as an official to the interim Iraqi civilian council in 1920. Izat Pasha Al-Kirkukli was responsible for the Ministry of Health and Education before becoming Minister of Public Works after the appointment of King Faisal. However, in November 1921, just three months into Faisal's rule, Al-Kirkukli resigned from his post in protest at the manner in which the Turkmen minority was being discriminated against. Ironically his resignation fell on deaf ears and did nothing to bring about reform. This was the last time a Turkmen held such a high office in Iraq's government.

On May 4, 1924, the British garrison invoked the wrath of the Turkmen when what was intended to be a show of force in Kirkuk turned into a massacre. Under the command of British officers, locally recruited Arab mercenary troops, known as levies, marched into the central market square to disperse a gathering crowd of Turkmen protestors. A brawl suddenly erupted and the British soldiers fled the scene, fearing for their own safety. With the loss of control the ill disciplined levies soon ran amok, looting shops, and firing indiscriminately into the crowd. Those individuals thought to be responsible for organising the Turkmen protest were hunted down in their homes and summarily executed by the Arab levies.

When word spread of this atrocity to the outlying Turkmen villages, the British ordered the local police forces to impose a strict curfew to prevent a vigilante mob from entering Kirkuk and a further escalation of the violence. Desperate to restore calm to the area, British aircraft began dropping leaflets printed in Turkish urging the residents to remain calm and to exercise restraint. However, the outrage and anger of the

Turkmen could not be so easily contained. Even after a committee was established to assess the damage caused by the
rampaging levies and some compensation was paid to the victims the mood remained ugly towards the British military. The
Turkmen attitude towards the monarchy was also beginning
to sour.

In 1933, only one year after achieving Iraq's nominal independence, Faisal died and his playboy son, Ghazi, ascended
the throne. Although he enjoyed a lavish royal lifestyle, King
Ghazi nevertheless understood the politics of oil. In 1938, he
became the first ruler of Iraq to lay claim over Kuwaiti territory. Not by coincidence, this was the same year that oil was
discovered in the sheikdom of Kuwait. However, with both
states still under British military protection, Ghazi's attempted
annexation of Kuwait was easily thwarted through international diplomatic pressure. In 1939, when Ghazi was killed in
a suspicious automobile accident, many Iraqis believed that
the British secret service was responsible. Upon Ghazi's death,
his three-year-old son, Faisal II became king and the actual
ruling power in Iraq was in the hands of the boy's uncle, Abdul
Illah, who served as regent.

With a power vacuum in the absence of a strong ruler, the
Iraqi general staff exerted much more political influence
throughout this period. Although many were trained by the
British, several senior military officers resented the presence
of foreign soldiers on Iraqi soil.

When the Second World War erupted in Europe in September 1939, Abdul Illah, the ruling regent, did not declare his
support for Britain even though Iraq was technically a British
protectorate. With anti-British sentiment running high, Iraq
initially adopted a neutral wait-and-see position. However, by

March 1941 the fortunes of war had definitely shifted in Germany's favour. Adolf Hitler's Wehrmacht had blitzkrieged its way across western Europe, knocking France out of the war and pushing the British back across the English Channel. With America still adopting an isolationist position, Prime Minister Winston Churchill fought on against the Axis powers alone, trying to defend the far-flung British Empire on a number of fronts.

At this crucial juncture, a number of pro-German officers in the Iraqi army staged an uprising in Iraq. Under the leadership of Rashid Ali, what started as a military coup quickly degenerated into chaos as troops still loyal to the monarchy sought refuge in the British military bases.

Adil Muratli, who was attending teachers college in Baghdad at the time of the coup, remembers: "Although we had no formal military training, the decision was made to arm the students. The so-called rebels did not have enough troops to secure the streets. And with the British and Royalist units withdrawn from Baghdad, the looters threatened to overrun the city." Muratli, 18 years old at the time, soon found himself equipped with a Lee-Enfield rifle and a box of cartridges mounting nightly patrols with his classmates.

It did not take the British long to respond to the rebellion as it posed a threat to its vital wartime supply of oil. Before the Germans could exploit the situation and move to support the rebel Iraqi officers, the British began redirecting troops into Iraq. An Indian Army division en route to North Africa was hastily diverted to the port of Basra, and a British armoured column from Palestine was dispatched to reinforce the Iraqi garrison.

"One week after the rebellion began, the British planes returned to bomb the petrol dump in Baghdad," said Muratli. "While it did not cause many casualties among the rebels, it was enough of a demonstration to break the will of the mutineers—they simply melted away at that point and the British troops returned with little resistance."

Once order had been restored those responsible for the insurrection were quickly rounded up and tried as traitors. The ringleaders were summarily executed and the infant King Faisal II's monarchy was restored to power.

Despite the lack of resolve shown by the conspirators and their followers, the anti-British, anti-royalty movement continued to grow throughout Iraq, and those responsible for the March 1941 uprising would subsequently be regarded as martyrs by those who wanted real independence from colonial rule.

Although the Turkmen leaders and activists had not openly supported the Rashid Ali coup, their public influence was seen as a potential threat to future stability by the badly shaken Iraqi monarchy. As a result, a number of prominent teachers and intellects were forcibly removed from Turkmen communities in the north and relocated to cities such as Nasiriya and Basra in the south, where their influence among the Shiite Arabs would be completely neutralized.

After finishing his studies in Baghdad, Adil Muratli returned to Kirkuk and began teaching grade school. Although he was not politically active, he remembers that a number of his colleagues were rounded up during this period by the national police and only much later learning of his friends' forcible deportations to the south. On November 20, 1945, a 23-year-old Adil married. The Second World War was over, and with the oil riches being pumped out of Kirkuk, regardless of the political situation, things appeared to the young teacher to be going rather well. However, the oil workers, primarily Turkmen were being poorly paid by the British Petroleum company (BP) and this discontent manifested itself in the formation of a union. In early July 1946, union leaders ordered a general strike and oil production in Kirkuk ground to a halt. At the request of the British authorities, the Iraqi police force was instructed to break the strike. Unfortunately, the situation quickly degenerated into a bloodbath.

"Many of [the Turkmen residents] had marched in support of the Oil Workers Union to show our solidarity with their demands for a fair wage," said Adil Muratli. "When the police came, they didn't hesitate. They simply started firing into the crowd and we ran for our lives."

Dozens of Turkmen oil workers were killed and dozens more wounded in the one-sided exchange. In the aftermath, the Turkmen of Kirkuk were horrified at the senseless carnage and the British were apparently equally shocked at the ruthlessness of the Iraqi police. Although BP had originally ordered all striking workers to be expelled, in the wake of the massacre they instead chose to cut a deal with the union to allow everyone involved to return to work. Compensation was paid to the families of the victims, and a government board of inquiry was established to probe into the actions of the police. In the end, a few show trials were conducted but none of the officials responsible for the deaths was ever held accountable.

Over the next decade, tensions continued to simmer between the Turkmen and the central government in Baghdad. In 1950, the Directorate of Education in Kirkuk issued an official order which prohibited the use of the Turkish language in Turkmen schools. By this time, Adil Muratli had risen to the position of headmaster at the Kirkuk grade school. "It was their intention to force us to use Arabic as they felt this would ultimately be a unifying policy for all of Iraq," said Muratli. "However, it was not so easily accomplished in practice, as all of our training aids and textbooks up to that point were published in Turkish." The official crackdown on the use of Turkish resulted in creating a climate of fear for the Turkmen. In addition to an escalation in incidents of individual harassment, in 1954 Arab nationalists raided and burned the contents of a Turkish bookstore in Kirkuk.

By the time King Faisal II conducted the national census in 1957, the majority of the Turkmen population was already feeling oppressed by the Baghdad authorities. Many of the Turkmen who participated in the process filed false returns by listing themselves as Arabs to avoid further persecution. Prior to and during the census, leading Turkmen activists were seized and interrogated by the police. Gathering places frequented primarily by Turkmen nationalists, such as cafés and clubs, were either shut down or kept under surveillance in an effort to intimidate them. The efforts were largely successful as the official census record shows just 137,800 registered Turkmen.

However, the Turkmen were not the only ones weary of the political situation, whereby King Faisal II imposed British policy in exchange for military protection. By 1958, the quest for independence had manifested itself into a popular movement led by Abdul Karim Kassem. Once ignited into open revolution, the troops loyal to 23-year-old King Faisal II offered little resistance. Kassem quickly secured power, declared himself prime minister, pronounced Iraq to be a Republic and ordered the execution of Faisal and his top officers.

At this point the ties to Britain were officially cut. After policing the unfriendly territory of Iraq for four decades, the British were only too willing to close down their installations and hand over control to Kassem's troops.

The Turkmen of Iraq had actively supported Kassem's July 14 coup and hoped that in the wake of colonial rule a new order could be established wherein all ethnic groups received equal opportunity and representation. To demonstrate their support of the new President, tens of thousands of Turkmen deliberately ignored the existing curfew and drove to Baghdad from Kirkuk, Mosul, Erbil, Talafar, Tuz, Khurmatu and numerous smaller villages. As this convoy converged on the Iraqi capital, organisers directed the columns of vehicles into staging areas from which they marched en masse to the Ministry of Defence building.

Abdul Kassem welcomed the crowd of Turkmen, and received their leaders inside the main hall of the Ministry. Playing to the assembled crowd, the self-appointed prime minister assured the Turkmen that the 'new Iraq' would be a Utopian world where "all ethnic groups in Iraq were brethren and the Turkmen would be given every consideration by the new regime to enable them to enjoy full citizens' rights." As proof of his sincerity to respect the Turkmen minority, Kassem released the previously suppressed census data which showed their actual numbers to be 567,000. Encouraged by these developments, Turkmen intellectuals began to publish their own weekly newspaper in both Arabic and Turkish entitled *Al-Bashir* ("The Bringer of Glad Tidings").

However, the honeymoon between the newly liberated Turkmen community and Kassem's administration did not last long. To complicate matters, trouble also started brewing between the Turkmen and rival Kurdish warlords. This ethnic friction was destined to bring matters to a violent climax.

One of the first clashes occurred on October 25, 1958, when Mulla Mustafa Barzani, a Kurdish tribal chief insisted on entering Kirkuk. Turkmen mobs protested his arrival but the tension between the groups grew and street fights broke out between Barzani's Kurdish followers and the Turkmen. During the riots, Major Hedayat Arslan, the popular Turkmen commander of the military police, suffered a massive heart attack and died. Although it was not directly caused by the Kurds, the Turkmen blamed Barzani for the death and staged four days of massive protests to demonstrate their anger.

At the same time, the communist movement was sweeping across Iraq, unions were gaining political power and Abdul Kassem was having difficulty keeping his own military officers under control. And he had to contend with outside interference. While Britain had relinquished its interested in both Iran and Iraq, the United States had quickly moved in to fill the void and secure future oil supplies. Immediately following the British withdrawal from Iran in 1953, Prime Minister Mohammed Mossadegh had declared his country to be a republic. The Central Intelligence Agency (CIA), however, had a different agenda. At the urging of the United States, the Shah of Iran, Mohammed Reza Pahlavi, overthrew Mossadegh's fledgling republican government and placed himself atop the Iranian throne. Thanks to billions of dollars in U.S. weaponry and training for his army, the Shah of Iran would remain in power until 1979.

Although its control over the Shah was secure, the U.S. wanted to hedge its bets when it came to maintaining oil sources. When Kassem seized power in Iraq in 1958, the CIA established a covert cell known as the "Health Alteration Committee." In addition in plotting Kassem's assassination, the American conspired with their Turkish counterparts on a number of military contingency plans. Dubbed *Operation Cannonbone*, a joint U.S.-Turkey task force was to invade northern Iraq and seize the oilfields should a disruption in Iraqi oil exports ever occur.

One of Kassem's key initiatives was the development of the international association which became known as Organization of Petroleum Exporting Countries (OPEC). This vital commodity cartel held its first meeting in Baghdad in September 1960. Such a development was obviously not considered to be in America's long-term best interest.

Against this explosive international backdrop, Kassem's regime faced a more serious challenge from within. Following an aborted coup attempt, Nadhim Al-Tabakchil, the commander of the 2nd Army Division in Kirkuk was relieved of his command. His replacement, Brigadier Dawood Al-Janabi, immediately initiated a crackdown on Turkmen nationalism. One of his first directives was to close down the *Al-Bashir* newspaper—just 26 weeks after it had begun publishing. Under Janabi's instructions, the military police conducted weapons searches and seized the private arsenals of many Turkmen political leaders. Once again teachers and intellects were rounded up, many arrested and shipped off to Baghdad. The Kurdish communists were given a free rein by Al-Janabi, and they soon began a campaign of violence against the Turkmen of Kirkuk. Out of fear and frustration, a delegation of Turkmen sought an audience with Abdul Kassem in Baghdad to advise him of the deteriorating security situation in the north.

Armed with the propaganda pamphlets and hate literature that had been openly distributed by the Kurdish communists,

Kassem was persuaded to remove Brigadier Al-Janabi from power in Kirkuk. Although this move angered the Kurdish communists and the followers of Chieftain Mulla Barzani, Prime Minister Kassem personally assured the Turkmen delegation that their security was a priority. In June 1959, Kassem overturned many of the deportation orders that had been issued to the Turkmen dissidents, and they were free to make their way back to Kirkuk from their brief relocation.

What the Turkmen did not realize was that Kassem's promise of a safe environment was not being respected by the Kurds. On July 14, preparations were being made all across Iraq to celebrate the first anniversary of the new republic. Kassem's government had issued a decree urging numerous organizations and ethnic groups to participate as a show of solidarity. The Turkmen leaders responded by organizing a march through the streets of Kirkuk. Labour unions, civil service organizations, professional guilds and student groups all encouraged their constituents to attend the official march, while many other smaller associations planned their own general processions. However, as the ranks of the various parades converged at the head of Atlas Street, near the main marketplace, the Kurdish followers of Chieftain Barzani sprung their well coordinated trap.

Scattered throughout the Turkmen marchers were scores of Barzani's gunmen posing as demonstrators. At a pre-arranged signal, they threw down their banners and pulled out hidden firearms. As machine gun bullets ripped through the densely packed crowds the terrified people dispersed.

In the midst of the chaos, Kurdish assailants began to execute a methodical program of brutal assassination by searching out prominent Turkmen activists: many of these individuals were hunted down in their homes. The lucky ones were killed outright, while the unfortunate ones were dragged into the streets, their legs tied to the bumper of a car and then dragged at high speeds until their bloodied bodies resembled sides of freshly butchered meat.

Caught by surprise at the scale of the Kurdish attack, the local authorities issued a curfew, but there were too few policemen to actually enforce the directive. As the police and soldiers bunkered down, the Kurds continued to rampage throughout the streets of Kirkuk. Turkmen businesses were looted and burned, and both the landmark Atlas and Al-Alamain movie theatres were destroyed by mortar fire. With the entrances to the city blocked off, the carnage continued unabated for nearly three days. Although the military commander had notified Baghdad of the ethnic clashes and requested reinforcements, it was the heroic action of Abdullah Abdul Rahman that finally restored ordered.

At great personal risk, Rahman escaped from Kirkuk and travelled to Baghdad. Only after a personal meeting with Prime Minister Kassem was attained did the Iraqi ruler realize the gravity of the situation. Kassem then dispatched a brigade of infantry to Kirkuk. However, even after the soldiers arrived to help restore order, the Kurds continued to hamper efforts to bring the fires under control. Although they did not use their weapons on the soldiers, the Kurds blocked the streets and prevented fire engines and ambulances from entering the central square to clear away the now bloated, rotting corpses.

By July 18, order had been restored and the casualty count tallied. In total 25 Turkmen, most of them political activists, had been killed and 140 wounded. Prime Minister Kassem released photos of the mass graves and destroyed buildings and vowed to take harsh revenge against the perpetrators of the massacre. Describing the Kurdish attack as "barbaric," Kassem also expressed his condolences to the Turkmen people, whom he described as "peaceful and traumatized citizens."

A government commission was convened to determine who was responsible for the massacre. Many senior military officers testified that complicity had existed between members of the army and the Kurds, and that, at the very least, warning signs had been deliberately ignored. Nevertheless, the commission did not hold the government in any way accountable. Twenty-eight Kurds were later convicted for their part in the massacre and sentenced to death.

The 1950s and 1960s proved to be very turbulent times in Iraq, and Kassem had many powerful enemies. Following the unsuccessful coup attempt in November 1959—planned and executed by the CIA's "Health Alteration Committee"—Kassem drastically altered his position on the Kirkuk affair. Suddenly blaming the whole incident on Egyptian conspirators and the emerging Baath party, Kassem issued a pardon for all 28 Kurds that had been convicted of the Kirkuk riot deaths.

Destined to be short-lived, the chaotic rule of Prime Minister Kassem was toppled in a bloody coup staged by the CIA-sponsored Baathists in 1963. One of those responsible for ousting Kassem's regime was none other than a young Saddam Hussein. At the time, Saddam was seen as an up-and-comer in the ranks of the Baath party, and the CIA had been impressed by his charisma and intelligence. As soon as the Baathists established themselves in power, Saddam also impressed his CIA sponsors with his ruthlessness. Testifying about the CIA's involvement in the coup, one agent quipped to a U.S. Senate

Committee, "The target [Abdul Kassem] suffered a terminal illness before a firing squad in Baghdad." The CIA's Health Alteration Committee had accomplished its mission—the removal of Kassem from power in Iraq with the help of Saddam Hussein.

But the killing did not stop with Kassem's death. The Baath party rounded up hundreds of former military officers gave them a brief trial and summarily executed them the same day. Included in the list of those killed was Brigadier Dawood Al-Janabi, the officer who had allowed the Kurds and communists to intimidate the Turkmen in Kirkuk.

The newly installed Baathist regime also took measures to reinstate the original charges against the individuals responsible for the 1959 massacre and, on June 23, 1963, the 28 Kurdish ringleaders were put to death. While this gesture may have originally been viewed by the Turkmen as an encouraging sign that the new government would respect their cultural rights, it was actually something far more ominous. The Baath party realized that to remain in power in Iraq it would have to ruthlessly eliminate every potential political threat. Far from being the harbinger of new freedom, the Baath party's assumption of power signalled an even darker chapter in the Turkmens' history.

OPPOSITE PAGE, TOP: As Colonial Secretary, Winston Churchill advocated that the Royal Air Force use chemical weapons to subdue the Kurdish uprising of 1920. (BBC HULTON PICTURE) **CENTRE:** *Turkish troops* **(left)** *under General Pasha retained control of Mosul at the time of the October 1918 Armistice. However, when British troops violated the agreement and pushed north, Kemal Attaturk* **(right)** *ordered the Turks to withdraw without a fight.* **BOTTOM LEFT:** *Field Marshal Edmund Allenby, commander of the British forces in the Middle East during World War I.* **BOTTOM RIGHT:** *Iraqi President Abdul Kassem.*

ABOVE: Saddam Hussein, pictured in traditional Kurdish dress, became President of Iraq in 1979.
OPPOSITE PAGE: Under the Baath party's system of tribal patronage, minorities like the Turkmen of Talafar were impoverished through deliberate government neglect. (SCOTT TAYLOR)

Chapter Four
The Baath Purges

DURING MY NUMEROUS TRIPS to Iraq I had often heard about Saddam's policy of Arabification, and in particular his thirty-year program of forced resettlement of Shiite and Sunni Arabs to the north. While these stories were usually told in conjunction with descriptions of Kurdish and Turkmen families having been displaced to make way for the newcomers, I had never fully understood the cultural impact this policy had on the ethnic minorities that remained in their homelands, until I visited the Turkmen city of Talafar in June 2004.

It had not been easy to find the location of Iraqi Turkmen Front office—not because the building was inconspicuous, but because the residents were immediately suspicious of my driver, Anmar Saadi, and me. Although there are more than 400,000 inhabitants, there is not a single hotel in Talafar so strangers are a rare sight in this remote city.

Anmar had no difficulty in asking directions in Arabic, but

the Turkmen children he questioned had been reluctant to acknowledge the whereabouts of either the ITF, or Dr. Yashar Talafarli, our contact person. Only after we chanced upon one of Yashar's sons—and he confirmed that our arrival was expected—did their attitude change. Suddenly they couldn't wait to guide us to our destination, and we arrived at the ITF office surrounded by a dozen noisy school kids.

I had brought with me a number of copies of my recent book *Spinning on the Axis of Evil* (2003), which had just been published in the Turkish language.

As we waited for Dr. Yashar to arrive, I attempted to break the ice with the dozen or so Turkmen in the ITF office, by handing out copies of the book. Only one of them, Omar, spoke English and I felt that the book would help to bridge the language barrier and introduce them to my writing. I was surprised to see that while the Turkmen smiled appreciatively and glanced through the pages dutifully, they otherwise seemed disinterested. Sensing my puzzlement, Omar politely explained, "They cannot read Latin script." This was something I had not expected.

"But they do understand Turkish?" I asked. "Yes of course, but only spoken Turkish," Omar told me adding, "We have been taught to read and write in phonetic Arabic script, but the words we understand are Turkic dialect."

Over the past three decades, Saddam Hussein had effectively cut off the people of Talafar from virtually all access to educational resources. What they wrote in Arabic could not be read and understood by an Arab, and any Turkish literature written in Latin script could not be interpreted unless it was read aloud to them. Admittedly, Talafar is probably the most extreme case, as its population is entirely Turkmen. In other northern Iraqi cities where there is a substantial mix of Kurds and Arabs, the Turkmen have had far more opportunity to study and use other languages.

When Dr. Yashar joined us, he and his colleagues continued to discuss the evolution of the Turkmen dialect. "By pushing us to learn only Arabic, Saddam created a unique hybrid language," said Dr. Yashar, who was educated in English. "To learn Latin letters, even in the Turkish language, would still be a tremendous stepping stone to our young people learning other European languages."

With the passage of time, however, Turkmen wishing to further their studies in Iraq had no choice but to become proficient in Arabic. "In this manner, our best and our brightest would therefore be the first ones assimilated into the Arab world, while the rest of the Turkmen would be increasingly cut off from all outside written material," said Dr. Yashar. "Had they been allowed to continue Saddam's policy, the Baathists would have eventually extinguished the Turkmen language and culture in Iraq." However, such an outcome had not been immediately foreseen

~~~~~~~~~~

In March 1963, the Turkmen actually celebrated the ouster of Prime Minister Abdul Karim Kassem by staging a massive demonstration to welcome the Baath party's Revolutionary Command Council's rise to power. However, it did not take long for them to realize that the new regime had little room for Turkmen participation. Although members of the Revolutionary Council had met with a Turkmen delegation, their request to have at least one senior cabinet member appointed to

the new government fell on deaf ears. One attendee report-
edly pleaded with the Council by suggesting that the Turkmen would be satisfied with "even a minister of sewers and
hygiene."

Realizing that they were being denied representation, Turkmen student organizations decided to boycott the 1963 elections. The gesture would prove to be a hollow victory, as the
political vacuum created by the indecisive election results allowed Abdul Salim Arif, an army officer, to wrest control of
Iraq away from the Baathists.

For the next five years, it was back to the drawing board
for CIA-backed Saddam Hussein and his colleagues to try to
figure out how to get their party back in power. As the Baathists
plotted, schemed, and killed in their efforts to destabilize Abdul
Arif's administration, the Turkmen cause remained in political limbo. Although they were not officially supported, the
Turkmen were able to establish a number of cultural clubs and
athletic organizations—both in Kirkuk and Baghdad.

When the Baathists, under the nominal leadership of President Ahmed Hasa Al-Bakr returned to power after yet another
coup in July 1968, the Turkmen movement was quickly served
notice that its activities would no longer be tolerated. The
newly appointed Minister of Interior Salih Amash sent a letter
to the founding members of the Turkmen cultural clubs denying them continued approval to operate on the grounds that
"the law did not allow clubs or organizations to peruse covert
aims, detrimental to the authority of the regime." Although
the Turkmen protested and took their case before the Supreme
Court, they soon learned that, under the Baath party, the Iraqi
justice system was meant to impose control, not dispense justice. With the government order upheld, the Turkmen had no

choice but to shut down their clubs.

On January 6, 1969, the regime took matters one step further when they initiated yet another major crackdown against Kirkuk's leading Turkmen. Police swept through the business district in a full-scale manhunt for Turkmen activists. Many were arrested and hauled off to Baghdad, and the message was sent that this would be the fate of anyone engaged in activities which ran counter to Baathist policies. The following year the Turkmen were given a sense of false hope when the Revolutionary Command Council passed Decree No. 89 on July 24, 1970, which amended Iraq's constitution and formally acknowledged the cultural rights of the Turkmen people for the first time in their history.

Stating that it was the best means "for increasing the citizen's support and service to [Iraq]" the decree authorized the use of the Turkmen language as a medium of instruction in primary schools, and in all audiovisual media. Furthermore, Turkmen studies were to be officially recognized by the Ministry of Education, writers could form unions and were free to publish their works in Turkish, a directorate of Turkmen culture would be established within the Ministry, a weekly Turkmen newspaper could be published and there would be an increase of Turkmen programming on Kirkuk television.

For the long-suffering Turkmen, this proclamation by the governing body seemed almost too good to be true. And in fact, it was.

THE BAATHIST PARTY HAD granted minority rights as they wanted to appear to be in compliance with the United Nations Charter of Human Rights. While the UN resolution outlawing all forms of ethnic discrimination had been tabled on December 21, 1965, due to internal legal wrangling over the exact wording, the motion had not passed in to law until February 4, 1969.

After making two amendments—the first stated that Iraqi officials could not be held accountable in an international court for any breach of the Act, and the second claimed that by signing the document Iraq in no way recognized the State of Israel —the Revolutionary Command Council signed the United Nations protocol.

As an indication of good faith, the Iraqi government forwarded copies of its resolutions guaranteeing the Turkmen cultural rights, and similar documentation pertaining to the rights of Kurds and the other minority groups. While the Baath party presented this façade of goodwill to the UN, inside Iraq there was no real change and the "unofficial" policy of Arabification continued.

A poll taken after the July 24, 1970 decree which granted Turkmen cultural protection found that 104 of 124 schools in Kirkuk opted to teach classes in Turkish. The government, however, did not wish to recognize the situation and instead, ordered the Directorate of Education to pressure the parents and students into taking their lessons in Arabic.

In an effort to force the government to respect policy, on the six-month anniversary of the decree's passing, the Turkmen Brotherhood Club organized a gala fund-raising event. Staged at the Salahadin Theatre in Kirkuk, it was attended by a number of well-known Turkmen authors, poets, actors and political figures. The various speakers all hammered home on the same central theme: the reinstitution of their cultural rights and freedoms. The authorities in Baghdad were aware of the

TOP: *U.S. Secretary of State Henry Kissinger and President Richard Nixon. When the British withdrew, the U.S. increased its involvement in Iraqi politics.* (UNITED PRESS INTERNATIONAL) **ABOVE LEFT:** *The infamous Abu Ghraib prison, where Najmaden Uglo (above) was imprisoned by Saddam Hussein's Mukhabarat for seven years.* **LEFT:** *Anmar Saadi, a former soldier in the Republican Guard, served as guide and driver to the author on many trips to Iraq.* (SCOTT TAYLOR)

ABOVE: Adil Muratli through the ages—as a young schoolteacher studying in Baghdad, as headmaster of the Turkmen school in Kirkuk, and present day, as a pensioner living in Ankara, Turkey. (COURTESY A. MURATLI) **LEFT:** Tariq Aziz, Saddam Hussein's long-time Deputy Prime Minister, is an Assyrian Christian. Through a complex system of favouritism, Saddam divided Iraq's ethnic factions into a "coalition of guilt" in order to prop up the Baath party. **BOTTOM:** U.S. support for Reza Pahlavi, the Shah of Iran (with U.S. President Richard Nixon), could not prevent his overthrow in 1979 by the Shiite Islamic fundamentalist followers of Ayatollah Khomeini. (CORBIS)

event, and sensed that this sort of activity would only further ignite divisive nationalism. Instead of providing additional freedoms, the Revolutionary Council took immediate steps to reverse the concessions that had been made. The few Turkish language schools that had been in operation were closed.

Outraged at this clampdown, the Turkmen students mounted a series of protests. By November 1971, this had expanded into a full boycott of the education system by all Turkmen students. This move effectively closed the schools in Kirkuk, and the government seemed powerless to intervene. However, when the teachers union spoke out in support of the student strike, the Baath party could no longer ignore matters. Secret service agents and police swept through Kirkuk, rounded up the student organizers and arrested the entire executive of the Teachers Union. In the months that followed, more student leaders and activists were rounded up. The Revolutionary Command Council established a concentration camp on the outskirts of Baghdad to house "Turkmen dissidents," with the most troublesome of those arrested taken to the infamous Abu Ghraib prison, where torture was fast becoming a specialty of the Baath party's Mukhabarat.

During this time, a young Saddam Hussein quickly moved up through the ranks of the Baath party. While his uncle President Al-Bakr as the figurehead, Saddam was already regarded as the real power behind the throne. Although he owed his position to the CIA, which had helped sponsor and train him, Saddam did not remain beholden to the Americans. In fact, it was Saddam that took the lead role in nationalizing Iraq's oil in 1972, thus setting a trend throughout the Arab world which culminated in the 1973 OPEC oil embargo. In response to Saddam's "betrayal" of U.S. interests, the CIA placed Iraq on its list of countries it claimed supported terrorism which allowed the U.S. State Department to impose limited sanctions and economic reprisals. Meanwhile, the CIA began to concoct ways to destabilize its Baath regime and replace the leadership with someone more pliable than Saddam.

One of the means used to accomplish this was the covert arming and equipping of Kurdish warlords in northern Iraq. The Baathists had not played favourites when it came to imposing their Arabification policy, and the Kurds, like the Turkmen, felt that they were being culturally and politically oppressed. Chieftain Mulla Mustafa Barzani had since passed over his tribal leadership to his son Massoud. Barzani and Jalal Talabani, the head of a rival Kurdish clan from northeastern Iraq, were wooed by CIA agents who promised them arms and cash in return for assistance in destabilizing the northern provinces.

Equipped with the U.S. weaponry and training, the Kurdish peshmerga militias initiated a guerrilla offensive against the Baath party regimes. The Kurds naively assumed that American promises of an independent Kurdish homeland were genuine and achieved limited success against the government forces. They would soon realize that they had been nothing more than pawns of the U.S. State Department.

After enduring several years of bloody Kurdish insurrection, the Baghdad regime had been forced to the international bargaining table in 1975. Saddam Hussein, as Deputy President, flew to Algiers to meet with U.S. State Department officials and Iranian government representatives. It was at this summit that the real issue came to light. The Americans had sparked the Kurdish uprising to pressure Iraq into an agreement that would allow the Iran shared access to the strategic

Shatt al-Arab waterway. Reluctantly, Saddam had agreed to the deal, which would help to facilitate Iran's oil exports to America. In exchange the U.S. and Iran both agreed to immediately stop supporting Kurdish guerrillas.

Deprived of their international sponsors and with Saddam given a free hand, the Kurdish rebellion was suppressed by the Iraqi forces. The defeat of their erstwhile Kurdish allies was viewed rather callously by the U.S. State Department as means to an end. Then Secretary of State Henry Kissinger best summed up the attitude towards the United States' betrayal of the Kurds with the phrase "covert operation should not be confused with missionary work." The Americans had deliberately set up the Kurds in order to keep the price of oil from rising

IN 1979, SADDAM HUSSEIN was officially sworn in as President of Iraq, and from that moment on became all-powerful, albeit with the official sanction of the Baath party and the Revolutionary Command Council. To keep the lid on Iraq's diverse and fractious population, Saddam developed an elaborate system of patronage.

At the top of the pyramid were the extended members of his own Sunni Arab clan known as the Al-bu Nasir. Consisting of approximately 30,000 people, Saddam's "family" was based in his hometown of Tikrit. While these individuals were promoted to the top ranks of the civil service and military, secondary positions were awarded to other tribes from Tikrit— the Al-Tikritis and Sunni Arabs. Saddam also hand-picked a few select individuals as representatives of the various ethnic groups to serve in his inner Cabinet. (For instance, Tariq Aziz,

Iraq's long-standing Deputy Prime Minister under Saddam, is an Assyrian Christian from Mosul.) By keeping the majority Shia population resentful of the Sunni Arabs and marginalizing other minorities, like the Turkmen, Saddam was able to create what some Middle East experts describe as "a coalition of guilt"—the great fear among his privileged appointees was of what would happen should he be toppled.

Saddam was also not averse to ruling with an iron fist. Within weeks of assuming the presidency, his agents moved decisively against the Turkmen leadership. Anxious to stamp out all vestiges of the Turkmen nationalist movement, activists were once again rounded up, but this time Saddam went beyond jail and torture. Held without bail or even formal charges for nine months, retired Brigadier-General Abdullah Abdulrahman and Dr. Redha Demirchi were summarily executed on his orders.

It was during the 1980 wave of arrests that Najmaden Kasa Uglo was first seized by the Mukhabarat. Then a young man of 24, Najmaden was certainly not regarded as an intellectual—he had not even completed grade school—but he was seen as a devoted Turkmen nationalist. Najmaden would spend the first twelve months of his seven-year captivity locked in the infamous cells beneath the Mukhabarat headquarters in Baghdad. He endured almost continuous torture, including being forced to sit for hours in a tiny chamber that had nails in the walls to prevent the prisoner from leaning.

"When they would take us back to our cells you could not even walk because there was no circulation in your limbs," recalls Najmadan.

In spite of this, Najmaden refused to give up the names of his colleagues. He was eventually transferred to the Abu

Ghraib prison, where the Mukhabarat tried to convince him to work for them as a double agent. Although Najmaden steadfastly refused to cooperate, the Mukhabarat were able to recruit others within the Turkmen population and were thus able to establish the same climate of fear that prevailed in the rest of Iraq. Even in the entirely Turkmen enclave of Talafar, the Mukhabarat had little difficulty in establishing networks. "During that period, I was afraid to even confide things to my own brother," explained Dr. Yashar, a leader in the Talafar community. "They were very poor times and people would sell out their friends just to feed their families. It was a terrible experience."

It was about this time that Mukhabarat agents paid a personal visit to Adil Muratli. As the headmaster of the Kirkuk grade school, he was again instructed to cease all classes taught in the Turkish language. Threatened with physical violence if he refused to comply, Muratli, at the age of 59, opted for early retirement rather than give in to the Mukhabarat.

In response to this complete clampdown, many Turkmen nationalists decided to flee from Iraq. While organizations such as the Iraqi Turkmen Front would later establish themselves in exile, individuals like Dr. Yashar continued to work clandestinely in Iraq. "There was admittedly very little we could do. We could not organize protests because we ran the risk of arrest," he recalls. "Even to be discovered as a member of the ITF could lead to execution." As Saddam tightened his hold on the people of Iraq, events were taking place that would have a tremendous impact on all Iraqis.

In February 1979, the Shah of Iran, Muhammed Reza Pahlavi, was toppled from power following a bloody insurgency. True to their old friend, the U.S. State Department had supported the Shah's military right up until the end. Although it had long been recognized that the Shah had lost the support of the people, his security forces had used brutal methods to keep him in power. It is estimated that in his final year alone, the Shah's security forces killed over 45,000 suspected insurgents. In the end, the royalists were defeated by the mobs led by the fundamentalist cleric Ayatollah Khomeini. The Shah was forced into exile.

Relations between the new Iranian regime and the U.S. had immediately soured, and the tenuous relationship was further exacerbated in November 1979, when Iranian religious students stormed the U.S. embassy in Tehran and seized American diplomats and workers as hostages. As the whole world watched to see what U.S. President Jimmy Carter's reaction would be, all of a sudden Saddam Hussein found himself once again regarded as the darling of the U.S. State Department. United States National Security Advisor Zbigniew Brzezinsky publicly urged the Baghdad regime to attack Iran and dispose of the fundamentalist ayatollah. In return, Saddam was promised that the U.S. would recognize Iraq's sole ownership of the Shatt-al-Arab waterway and his nation would be taken off the CIA list of countries it claimed supported terrorist organization.

It was a tempting offer and Iran appeared to be ripe for the picking. As one of their first official acts, the Khomeini regime had put to death most of the Shah's former military officers. Although the new government had taken possession of the Shah's impressive arsenal of military hardware, the former Iranian rebels did not have the technical skills to employ sophisticated weaponry like fighter jets and helicopter gunships. And without access to U.S. suppliers for spare parts, they would soon be rendered useless. Saddam, on the other hand, had been steadily building up Iraq's military forces, and he fancied himself to be a master strategist.

So, after careful deliberation, Saddam accepted the U.S. offer. In 1980 Iraq invaded Iran and war became a way of life for Iraqis.

ABOVE: *When Saddam Hussein sent his troops into Iran in September 1980 he had no idea that it would spark nearly two decades of continual conflict. (U.S. ARMY)*

ABOVE: *The remnants of Saddam Hussein's shattered army litter the road from Kuwait to Basra in February 1991. (E. ADAMS/CORBIS SYGMA)*
OPPOSITE PAGE: *Two decades earlier, it was a much different picture when Iraqi soldiers first marched confidently to war against Iran. (WIP)*

Chapter Five
Gulf Wars

ON THE NIGHT OF November 11, 1982, Corporal Yuksel Aga was summoned to the sandbag bunker that constituted his battalion headquarters. Once Aga and the other tank commanders were assembled, the colonel gave them some grim news. The next morning their unit was to spearhead yet another offensive against the Iranians. Equipped with obsolete T-54 Soviet tanks, Aga and his comrades were to try and breach the well-defended Iranian trenches and defensive works.

"At that point in the war, the morale in both the Iraqi and Iranian armies was very low," Aga recalls. "A lot of our soldiers were deliberately placing their limbs outside the protection of their bunkers and tanks, hoping they would get wounded just so they could go home."

When the war was declared between Iraq and Iran on September 22, 1980, Yuksel Aga, a Turkmen born in Kirkuk, was attending Agricultural University in Baghdad. Despite his post-secondary education, Aga was conscripted as a soldier in a tank regiment. "There were very few non-Arabs selected as officers," explains Aga. "After attending the basic course at the tank training school in Tikrit, we were rushed into the front lines—and we stayed there as long as we survived."

On the eve of the battle, the commander explained to his troops that an elite unit of Republican Guard soldiers had taken up positions immediately to their rear. Their task was not to support them, but to shoot any soldier who attempted to flee from the battle. "He also told us that wounded soldiers would not be brought out of the battle lines because they required four soldiers for each stretcher, and too many of our troops were anxious to volunteer for this duty in order to escape the slaughter," says Aga. "They wanted us to know that if we went forward we would fight and die, and if we tried to retreat we would be killed."

At dawn on November 12, Corporal Aga's tank rolled out of the protective earthworks and rumbled toward the Iranian lines. Artillery fire crashed around the advancing Iraqi units and soon the battlefield was a fiery cauldron of smoke, flames and terrifying confusion. Just metres from the Iranian trenches, an RPG-7 anti-tank rocket struck the turret of Aga's tank and exploded beside his head. Aga was nearly torn apart by red-hot shrapnel. Still conscious despite the searing pain from nearly 50 separate wounds, Aga was pushed out of the burning tank by his mates, and lay helplessly beside it.

The scale of the casualties on both sides was horrific and no emergency treatment was at first offered to the wounded in the field. Those that had survived the attack fled back to their own trenches, leaving Aga and hundreds of other wounded behind. "Whenever I regained consciousness, I thought of reaching over to the Iranian positions in order to surrender—their wounded were moaning just a few meters away. But I did not have the strength," he recalled.

Under cover of darkness, Iraqi stretcher-bearers were finally sent forward to seek out and retrieve their wounded. The first recollection Aga has of this ordeal was of being treated at an overcrowded desert hospital that was packed full of badly wounded Iraqi and Iranian soldiers. "The sound of their screams were horrible. There was blood everywhere and the soldiers were screaming out insults about both Saddam and Ayatollah Khomeini," said Aga.

Due to the seriousness of his wounds, Aga was only stabilized and given plasma before being evacuated to Baghdad for surgery. Unfortunately, the sheer number of wounded from the failed offensive meant that Iraq's medical facilities were full to capacity. "My wounds were so critical that the ambulance drivers actually took me to the Al-Uluwya Pediatric Hospital in search of an available surgeon," Aga recalls. "Eventually they found a space for me, praise Allah."

One of the first things the Iraqi surgeons told him was that they lacked the expertise to reconstruct his shattered arm, but that they would do their best to repair it. At the outbreak of the war, Saddam had made arrangements with the British government to send the most severely injured soldiers for surgery in England. However, after fifteen months of continuous combat, there were so many wounded that Iraq could no longer afford to do it. As a result of the botched surgery Yuksel Aga was handicapped for life, but he nevertheless considers himself lucky to have survived.

In the decade-long conflict known as the Iran-Iraq War, nearly one million Iraqi soldiers were killed. What Saddam had thought would be a short, successful campaign—with his well-equipped army and air force easily defeating the ragtag Iranian revolutionary fighters—developed into a protracted stalemate. In the first few weeks of the campaign, Iraqi armoured divisions easily pushed deep inside the Iranian frontier, brushing aside the lightly armed Iranian forces. However, what Saddam and the U.S. State Department failed to factor into the equation was the fanatical dedication of the Iranian Islamic revolutionaries.

"They would come at us in human waves, regardless of the slaughter we were creating around them," said Anmar Saadi, my driver in Baghdad, when he recalled his wartime experience to me one night. As a young 22-year-old conscript, Anmar had gotten his first taste of battle with an air defence unit. However, as the Iranian air force posed little threat, Anmar's unit, with its twin-barrelled 23-mm machine gun cannons, was instead deployed in an anti-personnel role. Facing a full-scale frontal attack by Iranian infantry, Anmar vividly remembers seeing the impact of the large-calibre shells tearing into the enemy formations.

"The bullets would literally blow off entire limbs in a pink shower of blood, and a single shot would penetrate more than one enemy soldier in their tightly packed ranks," he says. "What was frightening wasn't the scale of the carnage we created, but that the survivors just kept coming at us like the living dead. They truly believed that they would be transported straight to heaven if they were martyred in battle."

When Anmar's detachment ran out of ammunition it was forced to withdraw. "We took the breech blocks out [to prevent future use by the Iranians] and abandoned our guns. But we simply could not stop the human avalanche."

As the war went on, it was not only Iranian numerical superiority that took its toll on the Iraqi armed forces. As Iranian officers gained battle experience, they were further assisted by covert arms shipments from none other than the United States. Although Saddam had initiated the war at America's urging, his regime was nevertheless still seen as a regional threat, particularly as the Baathists promoted a pan-Arab platform that was vehemently opposed to the State of Israel. In the first weeks of the war, as Saddam's forces seemed likely to defeat Iran, U.S. Secretary of State Henry Kissinger suggested "It's too bad that they both can't lose." By carefully balancing the supply of arms and the purchase of oil, the U.S. tried to ensure that both did.

By 1984, the Iranian forces had managed to push the Iraqis back to their pre-war positions, and were poised to capture not only the vital Shatt al-Arab waterway but also the southern city of Basra. At this point, Saddam began having serious doubts about the value of continued fighting. But when he began sounding out a peace proposal with Iran, he soon discovered that U.S. President Ronald Reagan had other plans. Special Envoy Donald Rumsfeld was dispatched to Iraq to convince Saddam to continue the war with promises of increased military assistance from his country. Rumsfeld assured the Iraqi dictator that America would do "anything and everything" to ensure an Iraqi victory. This declaration of support also included the approval of the sale of chemical and biological weapons to Iraq by American companies. Under U.S. supervision, Iraqi gunners deployed clouds of mustard gas and nerve agents to thwart the massive Iranian offensive in the Shatt al-Arab marshes. However, the Americans were still intent on playing both sides of the fence, and chemical and conventional weaponry was also provided covertly to the Iranians. (The covert dealings with Iran, at a time when official relations between the two countries were suspended, came to light in 1987 when the political scandal known as the Iran-Contra affair was exposed.)

With neither side able to win a decisive victory, Iran and Iraq signed a peace deal on August 20, 1988. Although Saddam proclaimed this day a national holiday and celebrated the event as a "triumph over evil," the war had been a disaster for Iraq. In addition to the human sacrifice of nearly one million men, Iraq had gone deeply into debt. The billions of dollars owed for foreign arms purchases was so crippling that, at deflated world oil prices, Saddam's war-ravaged petroleum industry could only pump enough oil to cover its interest payments; most of Iraq's debt was held by the oil-rich Gulf states of Qatar and Kuwait. Although everyone knew that Saddam had initiated the conflict by invading Iran, once the tide had turned, the Iraqi president billed his war as being an attempt by the Persians to seize Arab lands.

Although they are not Arabs, the Turkmen, like all other Iraqi minorities, had no choice but to fight in the ranks of Saddam's army. Military service for all males was mandatory and the two years of service could be extended indefinitely in times of war. Despite the cultural oppression inflicted upon them by Saddam's regime, many of the Turkmen who fought in the Iran-Iraq War believed it was their national duty. Their country was at war and while Saddam may have been a tyrant, he was their tyrant and the situation was certainly preferable to that of having an Iranian fundamentalist carve up Iraq and seize the oil fields of Basra.

Many Turkmen proved to be natural soldiers and advanced

quickly through the ranks to achieve senior appointments that would have been denied to them in peacetime. But the Iraqi military often failed to make full use of the skills and training the Turkmen conscripts had acquired as civilians when they registered them for service at the local depots. As a result, Dr. Yashar, a medical student and qualified veterinarian, would spend the war in the ranks in a transport battalion. "For the duration of the Iran-Iraq conflict, our lives were essentially put on hold," said Dr. Yashar. "There was no real resentment because of this, because it affected almost everybody in the whole country. Enduring the war simply became part of our way of life."

Nevertheless, rank still had its privilege. And more often than not, those with privilege—rather than military accomplishment—still held the top ranks. "It was common practice for Iraqis with money to pay a poor person to serve their tour of duty in the army," explained Zahim Jehad, a Turkmen from Erbil who discovered an aptitude for soldiering after being drafted as a combat engineer. He rose quickly to the rank of brigadier during the Iran-Iraq War. "The officer corps was also very elitist and they were corrupt to the core," he recalled.

Even with the Iranians threatening to overrun southern Iraq, Jehad claims that most of the commanders were more concerned with lining their pockets rather than fighting the war. "Saddam Hussein and his Revolutionary Command Council were authorizing tremendous sums of money and, officially, the troops should have been well provided for; however, in reality things were much different," says Jehad. "Most units only had 50 per cent of their soldiers actually on strength while the commander would simply pocket the rest of the payroll. The other officers would collect 'fines' from those soldiers not serving and the sergeants would sell the soldiers' food rations on the black market."

Jaded by the corruption and poor conditions, it was a rather demoralized and disillusioned mob of veterans that paraded through Baghdad to celebrate their 'victory' over Iran before being demobilized to try and restore their civilian lives.

Within two years these same men would find themselves once again recalled for military service. This time, however, their enemy would prove to be much more powerful.

~~~~~~~~~~

Immediately following the August 20, 1988 ceasefire between Iraq and Iran, the U.S. military began drafting up a new set of contingency plans for the Middle East. Although the Cold War was still in full swing, the massive U.S. arms buildup under President Ronald Reagan was fast pushing the Soviet Union to the brink of bankruptcy. George Bush Senior was Director of the CIA and had been instrumental in exaggerating the extent of the Soviets' military capability in order to justify the decision by the U.S. to invest in the space-based nuclear shield known as "Star Wars." Prophetically, it was none other than a young ambitious CIA operative named Paul Wolfowitz whom George Bush the Elder appointed to head Special Project 'B,' the desk responsible for false intelligence files on the Soviets. In the late 1980s, knowing enough not to believe its own reports, the CIA determined that the threat Saddam Hussein posed threat to America's oil supplies was greater than that of the crumbling Soviet military.

As a first step in protecting those supplies, it was necessary for the U.S. to not only distance itself from Saddam's regime, but to demonize the very same regime that, until then, it had been supplying with covert military aid. In September 1988, just one month after the ceasefire was signed, Iraq's Foreign Minister Sa'dun Hammadi was invited to Washington. While Saddam believed this was to be a friendly meeting to discuss the reconstruction of Iraq, it was in fact a deliberately planned public relations ambush. Two hours before the scheduled meeting between Hammadi and U.S. Secretary of State George Shultz was to take place, photographs of the February 1988 gas attack in Halabja were made public to the White House press corps. The horrific images of bloated children's corpses had the desired effect, and when Hammadi approached the podium to deliver his prepared address he was bombarded with angry questions about the massacre. Unable to respond, the Iraqi beat a hasty retreat. No journalists questioned the U.S. State Department as to why it had kept this secret for more than six months (during this same period, the U.S. had continued to supply weapons to Saddam Hussein). The story was explosive enough, however, for the U.S. Senate to impose an immediate embargo on the sale of food and weapons to Iraq.

Meanwhile, Pentagon records reveal that by the fall of 1988 General Norman Schwarzkopf and his staff were already conducting large-scale computer war games based on the scenario of Iraq invading Kuwait. As events unfolded, this premise changed from the hypothetically plausible to the imminently probable. And the U.S. military was fully prepared to reverse such an action.

Economically vulnerable as a result of his massive war debts and the U.S. trade sanctions, Saddam was dealt another serious blow when, in the spring of 1990, the Kuwaiti government suddenly called in its $30 billion loan. This money had been loaned to Saddam at America's insistence in order to purchase the war materiel necessary in the struggle against Iran. Not only had they demanded full and immediate restitution from Saddam, the Kuwaitis were also simultaneously overproducing oil in order to keep the world price lower. The U.S. economy was locked in a recession and President George Bush Sr. saw rising oil prices as inhibiting economic growth. Accordingly, the U.S. diplomatically pressured the Kuwaitis to deflate the price of oil by ignoring the quotas established by the Organization of Petroleum Exporting Companies (OPEC) and flooding the market. To accomplish this, the Kuwaitis began slant drilling into shared Iraq-Kuwait oil fields along the Iraqi border.

These provocations proved impossible for Saddam to ignore. While his Treasury may have been empty, he still had the military hardware and massive conscript army to exercise his own brand of regional diplomacy. In response to Kuwait's actions, Saddam threatened to invade. By July 25, 1990, the Iraqi army had mobilized and its armoured divisions had massed along the Kuwait border. While the Kuwaitis were still refusing to concede on either debt repayment or oil production, Saddam wanted to be sure that the United States would not intervene and deliberately sought clarification on its position. U.S. Ambassador April Glaspie met with the Iraqi dictator in Baghdad and told him, "We [the USA] have no opinion on Arab-Arab conflicts, like your border disagreement with Kuwait…. [Secretary of State] James Baker has directed our official spokesman to emphasize this instruction." Naturally, Saddam understood this to mean that he had a green light. On August 2, 1990, his troops rolled into Kuwait.

TOP: *Religious clerics served as generals in the army of Ayatollah Khomeini* **(left)**. *Following the coup that ousted the Shah, Khomeini purged the Iranian officer corps of all professional soldiers. Saddam Hussein believed that his more disciplined soldiers* **(above)** *would sweep to an easy victory against the fanatical but ill-trained Iranian Shiite fundamentalists. Saddam was wrong.*

TOP: *U.S. President George Bush Senior (flanked by General Colin Powell and Defense Secretary Dick Cheney) orchestrated the first Gulf War to expel Saddam's army from Kuwait.* (WHITE HOUSE PHOTO) **ABOVE LEFT:** *A Tomahawk cruise missile is launched during Desert Storm.* (GETTY IMAGES) **ABOVE RIGHT:** *Canadian soldiers with 1CER observe the post-war oil fires in Kuwait.* (S. TAYLOR)

The Iraqi army faced almost no opposition as the Kuwaiti security forces fled rather than fight. In a matter of hours Saddam had annexed Kuwait. Most of the prominent Kuwaiti families had already departed for their European villas rather than risk being captured. There were a number of brief skirmishes in the streets as long-oppressed Palestinian and foreign workers took advantage of the Iraqi army's arrival to loot abandoned homes and settle scores with their often abusive employers. "Most of the soldiers called up for service in the Kuwait invasion did not resent being part of the operation," said Brigadier Zahim Jehad. "And it was not only Saddam Hussein who believed that the oil riches of this artificially created kingdom belonged to all the people of Iraq."

Most Iraqis were well aware of the diplomatic and economic pressures being applied by Kuwait, having heard about them in the media. As such, there was much support for Saddam's decision. The invasion of Kuwait was seen by many as a necessary measure, not just to restore national pride, but also to save the Iraqi Treasury from bankruptcy. Four days after the Iraqi military crossed into Kuwait, however, they ran into unexpected difficulties.

On August 6, the U.S. decided that it would take a position on Arab-Arab affairs after all. Taking the lead at the United Nations, President George Bush Sr. called for the General Assembly to pass a resolution imposing full economic sanctions against Iraq. While Saddam was taken aback by this sudden reversal in U.S. policy, the other shoe was about to drop. President Bush cited falsified CIA satellite photos to claim that the Iraqis had moved armoured units in Kuwait to the Saudi Arabian border. Although this was later proven to be patently false, Bush used this pretext to launch *Operation Desert Shield* and hundred of thousands of American troops were dispatched to the Persian Gulf. By implying that Saddam was out to conquer "all the Middle East oil," any critic questioning the rationale of sending U.S. troops to the Gulf was denounced as a "Neville Chamberlain" (a reference to the British Prime Minister who failed to restrain Adolf Hitler at the Munich summit of 1938 and who has since become history's poster boy for appeasement). George Bush Senior and his spokespersons thus succeeded in portraying Saddam Hussein as a potential Hitler bent on world domination.

To further demonize Saddam and the Iraqis in order to sway U.S. public opinion in favour of a war, a New York public relations firm concocted the famous "incubator lie." The elaborate fabrication included the emotional testimony of a young Kuwaiti woman who claimed to have escaped from her country after the invasion and witnessing "Iraqi soldiers throwing sick babies out of their incubators, and leaving them to die on the floor." It was emotionally gripping stuff, but it was also completely untrue. The fact that the media and the public had been duped by clever propaganda was only realized after the war. The so-called "eyewitness" was none other than the daughter of the Kuwaiti ambassador to the United States, and she been in Washington, DC, prior to and during the invasion. The lie worked, and suddenly American citizens who could not place either Iraq or Kuwait on a map were clamouring for war.

Although U.S. President Bush maintained that the massive military build up in the Persian Gulf was strictly defensive and aimed at curbing Saddam's potential aggression against Saudi Arabia, some of his senior brass were less coy about the plan. Air Force Chief of Staff General Michael Dugan was one of those who could not wait to let the cat out of the bag. He told the *Washington Post* that, in the event of war, the list of targets was topped by "downtown Baghdad."

In a further breach of military security, Dugan went on to claim his pilots were going to destroy "Iraqi power grids, roads, railroads, and domestic petroleum refineries." As a clue to Bush's true intentions, Dugan stressed that his air force "would not target the oilfields." The *Washington Post* interview had barely been published before Secretary of Defense Dick Cheney announced that General Dugan had been fired for making "inappropriate" comments. Despite official denials, it was becoming increasingly clear that a war between Iraq and a U.S.-led coalition would be unavoidable.

Military pundits in America took to the airwaves to try and portray this as a formidable challenge. With visual aids and graphics, they explained that it would be an epic struggle since a fully mobilized Iraq could field approximately 950,000 troops, nearly double the number of U.S. coalition troops deployed in the Persian Gulf. In terms of armoured vehicles, they said the Iraqi military possessed a staggering 5,500 tanks and 9,000 armoured personnel carriers (APCs), while the Allies only had about 4,000 tanks and a similar number of APCs deployed in theatre. Where the U.S. coalition held the edge, however, was in its massive array of 1,800 modern jet fighter aircraft and about 1,700 attack helicopters. According to reports, Iraq still possessed a respectable 160 helicopters, 700 fighters and a vast arsenal of air defense weaponry. Billed as the fourth-largest army in the world, U.S. pundits always added that Saddam's legions were "battle-tested" after their decade-long war against Iran. "We had no such illusions about our own capability," said Brigadier Jehad. "Everyone knew that if we went to war against the United States we would be destroyed."

BY JANUARY 17, 1991, the U.S. had assembled a coalition force from over thirty countries (including Britain, France and Canada) of 700,000 troops poised along the Saudi Arabia-Kuwait border and in the neighbouring Gulf States. When the UN deadline for Saddam's withdrawal from Kuwait expired at midnight, the allied air forces launched a massive attack known as *Operation Desert Storm*. Although the stated objective was to liberate Kuwait, most of the targets were actually inside Iraq itself. Just as General Dugan had predicted, American air power was used to bomb Iraq back into the Stone Age. While several low-flying allied aircraft were brought down, Iraq's air defense systems were for the most part of little use and the allied fighter jets struck with virtual impunity. Power plants, communications networks, government buildings, bridges, factories and even sewage and water treatment plants were systematically bombed and the Iraqi people suffered terribly from the destruction of basic utilities.

Although Saddam's envoys were desperately trying to negotiate a diplomatic face-saving compromise—at a meeting with the Russians in Paris, Iraq had agreed to withdraw from Kuwait in exchange for a ceasefire—it proved to be a case of too little, too late. At dawn on February 24 and following a sustained whirlwind of aerial artillery bombardment, allied tanks pushed northward from northeastern Saudi Arabia into Kuwait and southern Iraq. *Operation Desert Sabre* was underway.

"We had all believed that somehow Saddam would be able to negotiate a peace deal before committing us to a battle with the Americans," said Brigadier Zahim Jehad. "You can imagine our disappointment when we discovered ourselves under attack."

The battle turned out to be one of the most one-sided engagements in the history of warfare. Some Iraqis attempted to fight but most surrendered or tried to flee from Kuwait. Within 72 hours of the massive allied ground offensive, the vaunted might of the Iraqi army was totally crushed: Nearly 200,000 troops were killed, wounded or captured; 4,000 tanks were destroyed along with 2,140 artillery pieces, 1,856 armoured personnel carriers, 7 helicopters and 240 combat aircraft. Allied losses by comparison were amazingly light. Only four U.S. tanks had been destroyed by enemy action, while an additional artillery piece and 9 APCs had been put out of action by friendly fire.

In total, the U.S.-led coalition suffered just 148 fatalities during the conflict and the immediate post-war period. Approximately 31 per cent of the deaths were the result of friendly fire, and the majority of the remainder occurred when unexploded ordnance detonated during cleanup operations. Only a handful of soldiers were actually killed by Iraqi fire in combat.

The ease with which they had perpetrated this slaughter had surprised even the allied commanders. One of them later reflected that his peers should use caution when examining the results of this conflict. Major General Patrick Cordingley, commanding officer of the famed British "Desert Rats" armoured division, warned: "We must be careful about the lessons we take from a war where we defeated a technologically inferior enemy on featureless terrain and met very few reverses."

In his autobiography *In the Eye of the Storm*, General Cordingley noted that many of his soldiers had been "disturbed by what they had seen or done" during the battle. "The collapse of the Iraqi army was on a scale no one had anticipated... The Iraqis, without night vision [equipment], were at a terrible disadvantage; the only thing they could fire at was the flash of [our] muzzles, but they were out of range... as fast as they could pour vehicles in [we] destroyed them... The lucky few withdrew."

Even in retreat there was no safety for the Iraqis. As a trickle of fleeing troops became a flood, the highway from Kuwait to Basra became clogged with vehicles of all description. Allied aircraft pounded the columns of retreating Iraqi soldiers, and on the outskirts of Kuwait City they dropped massive bunker-buster bombs to crater the road. With the highway impassible, the planes dropped cluster bombs and air deployable land mines to extend the obstacle. Not realizing that their passage was blocked, the vehicles of the fleeing Iraqis joined those already backed up and unable to move forward. It was then that the allied air force struck in full force, turning the Basra-Kuwait road into the "Highway of Death."

Canadian CF-18 fighters based in Qatar were only equipped with air-to-air missiles, as their role was to provide rear area combat air patrols. However, upon hearing from allied pilots that there was a massive "turkey shoot" taking place in Kuwait, unofficial arrangements were made to equip the Canadians with U.S. bombs. One pilot recalled that "even at 30,000 feet you didn't have to find targets. The glow of the fires and the smoke clouds were all you needed to aim at."

Most of the tanks destroyed by the allies in Kuwait were older models—1954-55 vintage Soviet armour—because

Saddam had withdrawn his better-equipped Republican Guard units prior to the attack. Although they were primarily stationed inside Iraq, with many near Basra, these elite regiments were not impervious to the aerial onslaught and suffered heavy losses.

By the time U.S. President Bush declared a ceasefire on February 28, 1991, and the coalition withdrew its troops from Iraqi territory, morale and discipline collapsed in Saddam's army. Shiite fundamentalist clerics seized the moment to initiate a rebellion against the Baathist regime and Saddam was faced with an even greater threat in the form of internal revolt. As the embattled Iraqi president tried to rally his retreating divisions in the south, Kurdish warlords rose up in the north at the urging of the U.S. The Kurds quickly disarmed local garrisons in Dohuk, Erbil and Sulaimaniyah, and the peshmerga militias seized control of the streets of Kirkuk. In response, Saddam sent troops north, but they were of dubious loyalty as many of them were Kurds and Turkmen. Gilman Haja, a 24-year-old soldier at the time, later recalled that "when we were sent into the lines opposing the peshmerga, my Kurdish comrades and I took the first opportunity to discard our uniforms and switch sides."

The Turkmen also rejoiced at the prospect of ousting Saddam, and many young men took up arms and joined in the drive on Baghdad. Zygon Chechen, than a 41-year-old shopkeeper in Kirkuk, was one of them. "We believed that Saddam's regime had collapsed. And without his army to protect him it would all be over in a couple of days," Chechen recalled. "In the end, we had underestimated Saddam's survivability."

To crush the rebellion in the north, Saddam dispatched some

of his regrouped Republican Guard regiments and members of the Iranian mujahedeen Khalq. This elite fighting force had joined Saddam's ranks as exiles during the Iran-Iraq conflict. With the 1988 ceasefire they had become a stateless military force, some 10,000 troops with their own armour and artillery. For their loyalty in battle against Ayatollah Khomeini, the Khalq were granted land inside Iraq by a grateful Saddam. Now in his hour of need, Saddam called upon them and they responded with a savage fury in routing the Kurdish peshmerga. Assisting Saddam's ground forces, the Iraqi air force unleashed its attack helicopters against the rebels. With so many allied fighter jets in the Persian Gulf, the Kurds could not believe that the coalition forces would not intervene on their behalf. But as the Iraqi pilots pressed home their attacks, allied fighter jets flying high above them simply watched the action below. Realizing that they had been betrayed by the U.S., the Kurdish uprising collapsed.

Civilians and rebels alike, fearing the vengeance of Saddam's troops, began fleeing north. Zygon Chechen and his family were among those who packed up the few belongings they could carry and headed north. At repeated intervals, the fleeing refugees were strafed by attacking helicopter gunships. During one attack, Chechen's 14-year-old son was killed, and he had part of his left foot blown off. "Despite what we had just endured and suffered, the Kurdish peshmerga used this opportunity to rob us of all our remaining money and valuables," said Chechen. "They were pleading with the world to come to their rescue and save them from Saddam's wrath, and at the same time they were robbing Turkmen at gunpoint!" Chechen eventually received medical treatment at a refugee camp inside the Turkish border and from there he and his family eventually immigrated to Canada. Settling in Toronto, he would try to start a new life and put the war behind him.

Gaan Latis, at the impressionable age of 17 had also taken up arms and joined the Turkmen rebels. After he and his comrades were forced to flee, Latis vowed to continue fighting against Saddam from exile. Members of the Iraqi Turkmen Front put the young man in contact with the U.S. embassy in Istanbul. After being interviewed by "DOT" (the CIA), Latis began working at the U.S.-funded Radio Free Iraq Liberation. Although transmitting regular broadcasts in the Turkish language did not directly challenge Saddam's grip on Iraq, it did keep the hope alive for those Turkmen still enduring his rule.

ABOVE & LEFT: Yuksel Aga and his tank crew near the front lines during the Iran-Iraq War. Conscripted into service, Yuksel, like many Turkmen, had no choice but to fight for Iraq. To keep them at their posts, Republican Guard units were posted behind the Iraqi front lines. (COURTESY YUKSEL AGA)

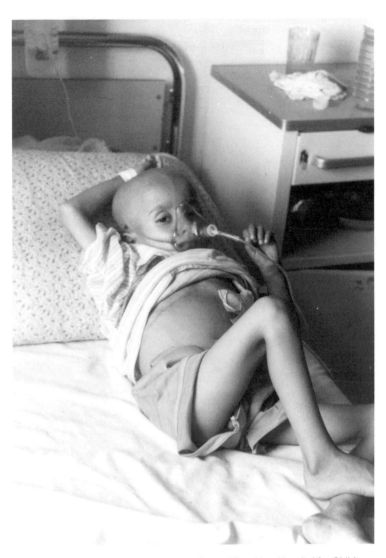

ABOVE: *A leukemia patient at Saddam Central Teaching Hospital for Children. Following the first Gulf War, nearly 500,000 Iraqi children died as a direct result of the economic sanctions imposed on Iraq by the UN.* (SCOTT TAYLOR)
OPPOSITE PAGE: *Iraqi women line up for their rations during the post-war famine.* (REIN KRAUSE/REUTERS)

Chapter Six
Sanctions and Suffering

IN MARCH 1991, as far as the Western world was concerned, the Gulf War was over: President George Bush Sr. had triumphed over Saddam Hussein; Kuwait was liberated; and the troops were returning home to a sea of yellow ribbons and welcoming crowds. Iraq's internal unrest, however, received scant media coverage other than to document the refugee camps filled with Kurds in eastern Turkey and northern Iraq.

While all of the U.S. soldiers had been withdrawn from Iraqi territory, a large American military presence was being maintained in the Persian Gulf. This coalition force purportedly remained in Kuwait as a deterrent to a possible Iraqi counterstrike which, in reality, could not have been mustered by Saddam's defeated army. In addition to the Americans, a large contingent of UN peacekeepers—including Canadian combat engineers—was tasked with monitoring the demilitarized zone between Iraq and Kuwait.

While I was in Kuwait to report on the activities of 1 Combat Engineer Regiment (1CER), I learned first hand of the U.S. complicity in allowing Saddam's troops to recover their abandoned equipment. Not only were Iraqi soldiers seen spiriting across the border at night to reclaim disabled tanks and artillery, the Canadians also found a battery of 17 Silkworm anti-ship missiles that was being hauled back into Iraq a couple of rockets at a time. As part of the UN mission, the Canadian soldiers' mandate was limited and did not include the securing of weapons; their job was simply to observe. The Canadian commanding officer, however, did advise his American colleagues of the abandoned missile site and of the fact that the Iraqis were sneaking in to recover the weapons. Obviously the Iraqis were still short of transport since it took them four nights to reclaim the entire battery. At no time did the Americans move to interfere with the Iraqi army's recovery operations.

By the fall of 1991, Saddam had managed to regroup enough of his armoured divisions to mount effective offensives against the last of the rebellious provinces. However, even as his security forces moved to punish the insurgents, the crippling economic embargo, which included all oil sales, had started to take its toll. The Iraqi dinar, which had traded at a pre-war value of $3.60 US, plummeted to the point where over 2,000 dinars were required to purchase a single American dollar—an incredible devaluation of 7,000 per cent. With the Iraqi economy in a free fall, even upper middle-class Baath party supporters suffered.

Prior to the war Iraq had imported approximately 30 per cent of its foodstuffs. The trade sanctions meant that many staples had become in very short supply. It was also impossible for Saddam's government to acquire many of the items necessary to rebuild the country's shattered infrastructure. In particular, the power grid could not be restored completely, and water and sewage treatment plants remained inoperable. Without access to potable water, many Iraqis turned to the desperate measure of pumping directly from the polluted Tigris River. Epidemics of water-borne diseases erupted. This, in conjunction with the shortage of food, proved to be a fatal combination. A simple case of dysentery often caused death among infants and the elderly as the vitamins and medicines needed to treat this disease were not available. Between 1991 and 1996, the United Nations estimated that 1.5 million Iraqis, including 500,000 children under the age of 12, died as a direct result of the U.S.-imposed sanctions.

"I can recall a night in 1995 when I had to put my children to bed hungry," said Jabar Abu Marwan. "I promised them I would have food in the morning, but I had no money and nothing left to sell." As an agent in the Mukhabarat many of Jabar's neighbours assumed that he enjoyed special privileges during the sanctions. "They didn't realize that we also had nothing; the government pay was nothing and the treasury was bankrupt. With no hope and no plan, I had gone on to my roof and began to cry. In fact I even put my pistol to my temple and cocked the hammer." In the end, he said that his love for his family stopped him from taking his own life. "If things were that bad with me trying to provide for them, what chance did they have with me gone?"

A slight reprieve came in 1996, when the UN recognized the scale of the human tragedy it was creating as a result of the trade embargo. In order to 'relax' the sanctions, the UN Security Council drafted a policy that would allow Iraq to export certain quantities of oil in exchange for the purchase of basic foods items and medicines. Although agreed to in principle in May 1996, the first shipments under this new arrangement were not delivered to Iraq until March 1997, by which time the suffering of the Iraqi people had become acute.

Under the terms of the oil-for-food program, all revenue from Iraq's oil production was paid into an escrow account managed by the UN in New York. Thirty per cent of the revenue was automatically deducted and paid into the Kuwaiti Reparation Fund, a further three per cent was claimed as an operating expense for UN administrators, and a one per cent fee was charged by the UN's Banque Nationale de Paris. The remaining 66 per cent was divided again: 13 per cent was allotted to the three Kurd-controlled provinces in the north, with the balance of 53 per cent going to Saddam's government.

In Baghdad, I conducted several interviews with many UN officials responsible for the administration of the oil-for-food program. All of them were consistently critical of the UN Security Council's policy. One spokesman explained to me that "the 30 per cent paid to Kuwait is potentially in perpetuity because there is no fixed final sum." As long as the U.S. continued to mount air patrols over the no-fly zones they imposed over post-war Iraq, the mounting costs continued to be added to the bill. "Essentially, the U.S. used Iraq's oil exports to cover their cost of bombing Iraq."

It was also clear that the three per cent administration fee charged by the UN added up very quickly when it was applied to billions of dollars of controlled Iraqi exports. Between 1996 and 2000, the UN pocketed over $600 million US from the oil-for-food program. This unforeseen windfall certainly helped stabilize the perpetually cash-strapped organization and explains why no one in the UN Secretariat was eager to discontinue the sanctions.

With strict controls placed on all of Saddam's purchases, the Iraqi dictator had no real say in establishing the country's priorities. As a result of Security Council vetoes, much of the equipment needed to operate Iraq's oil industry could not be imported. Without the proper components, it became increasingly difficult to produce enough oil to meet the country's approved quota of oil exports.

Although the primary objective of the UN program was the distribution of food, even after it had been fully established a shortfall in many basic requirements remained. The same ration card was distributed to everyone, regardless of social status or profession. This card entitled the holder to the six basic items: rice, flour, sugar, tea, vegetable oil and chickpeas. A separate milk ration card was issued for infants and nursing mothers, but there was no allotment for meat or vegetables, which had to be purchased by the poorly paid Iraqi people with their virtually worthless dinars.

In the summer of 2000, when I first visited Iraq, the UN oil-for-food program was in full swing and the humanitarian crisis had been somewhat checked. Things were still very difficult, but the program had "stopped the decline," said George Somerwill, a former Canadian Broadcasting Corporation (CBC) journalist I had interviewed. Like many of his colleagues, Somerwill stressed that the aid program was receiving the full cooperation of the Iraqi regime. "We are granted access any time we request it, in order to follow up on the delivery process of goods. There was never any attempt by the Iraqis to divert any of the shipments for military purposes," said Somerwill. "Saddam knew enough not to deliberately starve his people if he wanted to remain in power."

Many Iraqis who endured the hardships of the sanctions believe that the oil-for-food program actually helped to prop up Saddam, rather than weaken his regime. "The people knew that the shortages from the embargo were the responsibility of the Americans and the British," said Dr. Yashar, director of the Iraqi Turkmen Front in Talafar. "Hungry people are docile and easily manipulated, whereas starving people become desperate and therefore uncontrollable."

That is not to say that a quiet resentment towards Saddam wasn't simmering away below the surface. For those who fled the country, a movement to organize an opposition in exile began to grow. The Iraqi National Congress (INC) was formed. With its headquarters in London, the organization's funding is primarily provided by the U.S. State Department. Loosely associated with the INC, the Iraqi Turkmen Front (ITF) had established an office in Ankara, Turkey, and was headquartered in the northern Iraqi city of Erbil.

Although Erbil was nominally supervised by the UN as part of the 1991 ceasefire agreement with Saddam, this city was in fact under the control of warlord Massoud Barzani's Kurdistan Democratic Party. Because the international community maintained a presence in the region and the UN controlled the transfer payments to the Kurdish leader, the establishment of the Turkmen Front's headquarters in the city was tolerated but not welcomed. However, since Ankara had more reliable communications and provided easier travel access, the ITF conducted most of its administration and coordination from there.

Although one would have believed that the Turkish government would have actively supported the exiled Turkmen, the ITF did not receive much assistance from this source. "The Turkish government was anxious to keep the various Kurdish factions from Iraq on their side, so as to deny them from assisting the Kurdish separatist [PKK] movement in eastern Turkey," explained Dr. Mustafa Ziya, a former director of the ITF's Ankara office. "It was the Turkish General Staff (TGS) that helped the Iraqi Turkmen cause."

As the constitutional power behind the democratically elected Turkish parliament, the TGS operates almost as a separate entity, with a mandate to intervene if necessary in domestic politics should there be any move to reverse the 1922 secular reforms of Kemal Attaturk. The TGS, therefore, has the unique role of protecting democracy while at the same time overseeing the country's entire parliamentary process. Its primary concern throughout the 1990s was preventing a PKK insurrection. As much of the weapons, money and administrative support for the PKK's guerrilla forces were channelled through northern Iraq, it was natural that Turkish intelligence (MIT) wished to cultivate a network of agents to assist them, and the Turkmen of Iraq were willingly recruited for this task.

With the Mukhabarat operating alongside the Turkish MIT, British MI6, CIA, and Asaish (the Kurdish warlords' secret service), the three small northern provinces of Iraq were a hotbed of spies and political intrigue. Distrust between the factions continued to grow. Open clashes erupted between Barzani's KDP and his rival Jalal Talabani's Patriotic Union of Kurdistan (PUK), and the animosity between the Turkmen and the Kurds continued to fester.

"The Kurds are always making a big noise and demonstrating their military might by parading their peshmerga around their buildings," said Anmar Saadi, who, as a Sunni Arab, considers himself an impartial observer of the factional disputes in northern Iraq. "Despite all their posturing, the Kurds are actually afraid of the Turkmen. Without making a noise, the Turkmen are like cobras. They just wait and then pounce suddenly on their victims and then disappear. That is why the Kurds are so frightened." Anmar explained all this to me in February 2003 while we were being held as 'guests' of Massoud Barzani's forces in the KDP's mountain stronghold at Massif Salahudin.

The problem had started at the border checkpoint. Without having received permission from Saddam's Mukhabarat to travel outside of Baghdad, Anmar and I had nevertheless made the decision make our way north towards Mosul. Although we had been briefly detained in Kirkuk, the Iraqi authorities appeared more puzzled than alarmed at our presence and allowed us to continue our journey. When we arrived at the Mukhabarat office in Mosul, we boldly walked in and asked for permission to cross into Kurdish territory. Given that this was only days before the war was about to begin and U.S. troops were already conducting training exercises in Iraq's northern provinces, our request was a hell of a long shot.

The Mukhabarat agent miscalculated our importance and assumed that if we had gotten this far from Baghdad, without escort, we must have had 'special' clearance. Besides, why would an unauthorized journalist voluntarily enter a Mukhabarat office and expect to be granted a travel pass? The bluff worked better than expected, and within an hour we had driven to the bridge that marked the extent of Saddam's control. Although there was a long line of traffic, a cheerful Iraqi officer waved us to the front of the queue. "That was too easy," Anmar said as we drove across the bridge to the Kurdish checkpoint. "I can't believe they didn't even question us."

On the Kurdish side, however, our luck ran out. Not fully understanding the inter-factional tensions that exist in the north, I had willingly told the peshmerga captain at the border that I intended to travel to Erbil to interview Dr. Sanan Ahmet Aga. With no telephone connections between Saddam-controlled Iraq and the Kurdish zone, I had asked the officer if it was possible for me to phone ahead so that I could inform Dr. Aga of my arrival. As Aga was at that time president of the Iraqi Turkmen Front, my request aroused suspicion. A second Kurdish officer was summoned, this one wearing civilian clothes and, judging by his manner, an obvious member of the KDP's Asaish.

After a brief conversation, we were told to pull off the road and wait by our car. For the next five hours that is exactly what we did. The border guards were pleasant enough, bringing us water and tea, smiling and replying, "No problem" whenever I asked the cause for the delay. As we had intended to drive back to Baghdad that evening, I realized that we no longer had enough time to get to Erbil and back before the border closed at nightfall. It was only when I asked to have our passports returned to us that I realized we were not free to leave. "Someone is coming for you," the Kurdish secret agent told us. When I asked if it was someone from Dr. Aga's office, he laughed, and then said, "No. You will not be speaking to that traitor. You will be taken to Massif Salahudin."

Asaish agent Gilman Haja drove us to the KDP's mountain hideaway in a black Mercedes. Haja told us that he had deserted from the Iraqi army to join the peshmerga during the 1991 uprising. Not knowing how long we were to be held as 'guests' of the KDP, neither Anmar nor I were very pleased with this turn of events. Our arrival at the headquarters in Salahudin was greeted by a very cordial group of Kurdish civilians. Although at that time it was virtually impossible for any international media to gain access to this remote region, the KDP had constructed a new "public relations centre" complete with a freshly painted sign.

Seemingly disappointed to see only the two of us, Maraan Mirkhan, the KDP's official spokesperson, explained that "We are expecting a flood of Western journalists to arrive here in the coming weeks" and he urged us to inspect the new facility. Mirkhan added that "We provide access to the Internet, telephones, coffee—anything you like." However, when I told him that what I really wanted was an interview with Dr. Sanan Aga of the Iraqi Turkmen Front, Mirkhan ushered me into a small room where he quietly informed me that the Turkmen were "not good people" and that "Sanan Aga works with Saddam Hussein."

Realizing that I did not have much time to spare if I was going to get back across the border before dark, I cut him short and, wanting to make the most of this setback, asked him to explain to me exactly what the situation was with the KDP. "We fly our own flag and patrol our own borders at present, but ultimately we are still Iraqi citizens," he replied. These lines were the same well-rehearsed rhetoric the Kurdish leaders had used to play up to the international media. "We are not trying establish an independent Kurdistan; rather we will fight to unify Iraq," continued Mirkhan.

It was interesting to note was that while U.S. President George W. Bush and his administration were still claiming that a peaceful resolution could be negotiated with Saddam, the Kurds were under no such illusions. When I asked him about the likelihood of a war, Mirkhan had simply laughed and said, "It's guaranteed; the Americans will definitely attack—in March."

Eventually, the KDP authorities relented and arranged to have us taken back to the border. It was well after dark when we arrived, and the crossing had already closed on the Iraqi side. Not wishing to spend the night waiting at the Kurdish guard house for the border to reopen, Anmar and I decided to cross the bridge and take our chances with the Iraqi soldiers.

It was a decision that proved almost fatal. The border guards were startled by the sight of two shadowy figures emerging from the darkness and coming towards them and began to panic. They quickly cocked their Kalashnikov rifles and given the order to fire but a timely counter-order shouted by their commanding officer saved us from being killed. The officer was not very pleased because this disturbance had interrupted his supper. "We were expecting you earlier. The border is now closed." When we explained that we had been deliberately detained by the KDP's Asaish, he softened and reluctantly agreed to let us pass. "My dinner is getting cold" was his curt reply to our profound thanks.

~~~~~~~~~~

It was evident from my interview with Maraan Mirkhan that the U.S. was cooperating closely with both Barzani's KDP and Talabani's PUK; and he had made no attempt to deny the pre-war buildup of American troops and equipment. Although the presence of U.S. Special Forces in the Kurdish provinces was supposed to be a secret, news items relating to their operations were being broadcast nightly on Turkish television. I had also found out that the CIA was desperately trying to recruit exiled Turkmen into the ranks of a new Iraqi liberation army, which the American agency was assembling in a remote base in southwestern Hungary.

I had first learned of the CIA project from my old friend Laci Zoldi, the Budapest-based reporter. When the Hungarian government announced that the U.S. military would be using the air force base in Taszar to train Iraqi civilian "interpreters and guides," even the most naive of journalists would not believe the premise. After Laci and I decided to work together on this story, we managed to speak with a representative of the Iraqi Turkmen Front in Ankara. Dr. Mustafa Ziya confirmed that the CIA was in fact recruiting former soldiers and training a combat force to fight alongside U.S. troops in the invasion of Iraq.

In order to round out this story, and prior to heading back to Baghdad at the end of January 2003, I arranged a quick visit to Hungary. The plan was to hook up with Laci in Budapest, where we would be joined by a couple of my old Balkan colleagues: American reporter Chris Deliso and Australian journalist Sasha Uzunov, both of them based in Macedonia. Naturally, security would be very tight at this 'secret training camp.' But we also knew that most Hungarians were opposed to their government's participation in such a venture.

The CIA hoped to recruit and train at least 3,000 Iraqi expatriates to form the nucleus of a post-Saddam army. To achieve this total, they had pressured members of all seven parties that constituted the Iraqi National Congress (INC)—an exiled coalition with the aim of bringing Saddam Hussein and his Baathist regime to an end—to meet their quota. Dr. Ziya had been tasked with recruiting 400 Turkmen. Although the INC was

TOP: "Shock and awe" bombing of Baghdad, March 2003. *(JEROME DELAY/ AP)* **ABOVE:** The U.S. ground invasion met little opposition. *(U.S. ARMY)* **LEFT:** The toppling of Saddam's statue in Firdos Square on April 9, 2003, marked the end of an era. *(J. DELAY/AP)*

TOP: U.S. instructors in Taszar, Hungary, train Iraqi exiles. (SCOTT TAYLOR) **CEN-TRE:** U.S. troops moved quickly to secure the North Oil Company's facilities in Kirkuk. (S. TAYLOR) **RIGHT:** Following Saddam's removal from power, widespread looting erupted all across Iraq. (AP/ANJA NIEDRINGHAUS)

first briefed about the formation of this liberation army in October 2002, the official authorization for the funding was not approved until December. "We were given just two weeks to find suitable candidates," said Dr. Ziya. "And although the U.S. was offering to pay all travel expenses, a good salary and a $3,000 signing bonus for each volunteer, it was an almost impossible task."

One of the Turkmen that Ziya did contact was Asif Sertturkmen, director of the Toronto-based Canadian chapter of the Iraqi Turkmen Front. From the estimated 1,500 Iraqi Turkmen living in Canada, not a single volunteer could be found. "It wasn't something that our people wanted to participate in. Not only did we know that the Americans had enough soldiers to defeat Saddam on their own, we also were not sure of what intentions the Americans had for post-war Iraq," said Sertturkmen. "In the end, it appears that our distrust of the U.S. was warranted."

Although recruiting soldiers for mercenary armies is illegal by Canadian law, the CIA-sponsored Iraqi project did sign up an undisclosed number of Kurdish Canadian volunteers. When the INC confirmed this fact and the story first broke in the *Ottawa Citizen* newspaper, a number of former Canadian government officials questioned whether the operation had been clandestinely cleared by top-level bureaucrats in Canada's Foreign Affairs department.

"Unless this is sanctioned by our government, we can't permit covert military recruiting in Canada, even if 'friendlies' are doing the recruiting," said David Harris, former Chief of Strategic Planning at the Canadian Security and Intelligence Service (CSIS). "Within our frontiers, the Canadian State must always have a monopoly on the recruiting and control of any armed force, however loosely described."

While the Pentagon steadfastly maintained that the Iraqi recruits were to be used only as guides and interpreters, our visit to Taszar completely debunked that myth. From civilian workers employed at the U.S. army base we learned that nearly 1,500 U.S. Special Forces personnel had been transferred in to serve as instructors. Although squads of heavily armed U.S. military police prevented us from getting anywhere near the base in Taszar, we figured there might be another way of confirming our suspicions. We staked out the local striptease bar.

It had not taken long for the place to fill up with big, athletic-looking, shorthaired Americans in civilian clothes. All it took was a "Where y'all from?" icebreaker from Chris Deliso in his New England accent, a few drinks, and some shared war stories before we hit pay dirt. Lowering his voice to a conspiratorial whisper, one of the American soldiers asked, "Can you guys keep a secret? We're not really travelling salesmen. We're SF guys sent here to train a bunch of fucking Iraqis."

As events were to unfold, Iraqi expatriates proved to be equally disdainful of the CIA's private army. Dr. Mustafa Ziya admitted that he was able to recruit only 56 Turkmen candidates out of a quota of 400, including Gaan Latis, the young former guerrilla who had left his job with the Radio Free Iraq Liberation in Istanbul to join. However, many of the INC volunteers, having pocketed travel visas and a $3,000 signing bonus, just disappeared. Of those that did make it into the training program, many more found that the strict discipline of boot camp was not to their liking and simply quit. Only an estimated 80 soldiers actually graduated from the Taszar facility. On the eve of the war, the CIA reluctantly shut down the failed project.

This level of failure should have set off alarm bells in the White House as to the scale of their pre-war miscalculations. Even with U.S. money and training, the fractious INC could not find enough soldiers to make up a liberation army. "We [Turkmen] had our own post-war priorities that did not include serving in an American-funded security force," explained Dr. Ziya. "We knew we would have to protect our homes and territory from Kurdish peshmerga."

As the countdown to war accelerated, so too did the warning signs that post-Saddam divisions, particularly in the north, were becoming even more fractious. Although Hans Blix, Executive Chairman of the UN Monitoring, Verification and Inspection Commission (UNMOVIC), had delivered his final report on January 27, 2003, which virtually ruled out any possibility that Saddam possessed weapons of mass destruction (WMD), he asked for more time "to be absolutely sure."

The U.S. President had his own timetable, however. On the very day following Blix's report to the UN Security Council—and contrary to what had been stated—President George W. Bush cited Iraqi's "lack of co-operation" with UN inspectors during his State of the Union address as a reason for a military intervention in Iraq. Although U.S. Secretary of State Colin Powell subsequently failed to convince the UN Security Council to support their plan of attack, the war drums continued to pound at the White House. On March 10, the U.S., Britain and Spain issued a collective statement that they would take the "necessary action against Iraq," even without a second resolution from the UN.

Immediately following this announcement, Dr. Zalmay Khalilzad, the U.S. Special Envoy for Northern Iraq, called a summit meeting of Iraqi 'stakeholders' at the Sheraton Hotel in Ankara. It was here that I finally met Dr. Sanan Aga, who had travelled from Erbil as head of the Iraqi Turkmen delegation. Heavy set, with white hair, a long thick moustache and piercing blue eyes, the avuncular Aga vaguely resembled the Hollywood cartoon character Mr. Moneybags. He was very friendly and approachable, but his entourage appeared to be nervous and tense. I told him of the difficulties I had encountered when I tried to get past the Kurds to visit him in Erbil. "Consider yourself lucky that they did not shoot you," he replied.

Although they were on neutral turf in Ankara and surrounded by Turkish intelligence (MIT) and police, the assembled Kurdish and Turkmen factions eyed each other with simmering hate across the Sheraton lobby. With war imminent, they were all trying to gain an edge and curry favour with U.S. Envoy Khalilzad. From the Kurdistan Democratic Party, Massoud Barzani had sent his nephew Nechevan to represent him at the meeting. I spoke with Nechevan at length, and while he seemed content with what Khalilzad was promising as post-war spoils, he remained distrustful of Americans in general. "At the moment we share a common goal," said Nechevan Barzani. "But we Kurds have not forgotten that the USA sold us out in the 1975 Algiers agreement, and again in 1991 when they betrayed us to Saddam during the uprising."

The Turkish government used the occasion of the Khalilzad summit to reiterate that it would not allow the Kurds to seize the oilfields of Kirkuk as a step towards an independent Kurdistan. Government representatives also warned that they would not tolerate any discrimination against the Turkmen of Iraq. As a precaution—and to back up their bargaining condition—the Turks had begun positioning its 7th Armoured Corps along the border with Iraq. The Turkish government also announced that it was prepared to take unilateral action to secure northern Iraq militarily if its demands were not met. Without realizing the irony of his comments, President Bush responded that any "unsanctioned military incursion" into Iraq by Turkey would be considered "illegal" by the international community. For his part, Barzani, whose KDP controlled the area along the Turkish border, rejected Turkey's ultimatum with contempt. "If they want to enter our territory, I'm afraid that will have to fight their way past our peshmerga," declared the KDP delegate.

Despite the eleventh hour attempt to forge a binding agreement, Khalilzad failed to find common ground among the delegates in Ankara. The ITF's Dr. Sanan Aga summed up the U.S. position as "impossible, because they are promising everything to everyone in an attempt to forge an alliance against Saddam. However, after the war they will have to break some of those promises... and then we will find out who America truly supports." With no firm plan agreed to for northern Iraq, time simply ran out on Khalilzad and his diplomatic mission.

~~~~~~~~~~

On March 18, 2003, George W. Bush announced that he was running out of patience, and gave Saddam Hussein the ultimatum to abdicate his presidency within the next 48 hours "or else." Saddam didn't budge and on the evening of March 20, the U.S. and Britain launched a precision bombing attack on the outskirts of Baghdad. Although it was described by the coalition as a successful leadership strike, a visibly shaken but very much alive Saddam Hussein appeared the following morning on state television to denounce the attacks.

Within hours, coalition special forces and armoured columns began pouring into southern Iraq from jump-off positions in Kuwait. After the first few days of the campaign it became apparent that the Iraqi army had collapsed. Conscripts surrendered in the hundreds and allied troops swept through vast tracts of empty desert.

The strongest opposition to the coalition's forces came in the form of the irregular volunteers who called themselves the Fedayeen Saddam. Fighting as guerrillas, the Fedayeen managed to win a few skirmishes against the advancing Americans. The most notable of these was the March 23, 2003 ambush of Private Jessica Lynch's 507th Maintenance Company near Nasiriya. A total of 10 U.S. soldiers were killed in that battle, 50 were wounded and a further 12—including Private Lynch—were taken prisoner.

Despite the reversal, the U.S. vanguard had pushed close to the southern suburbs of Baghdad within 72 hours, and allied aircraft were pounding the Iraqi capital with impunity as part of its "shock and awe" bombing strategy. With reports that advance units of coalition commandos had been used to secure Iraqi oil infrastructures to prevent its sabotage, some reporters in Washington asked U.S. Secretary of Defense Donald Rumsfeld why the Americans had not used such tactics to secure the so-far-undiscovered Iraqi arsenal of WMDs. In response, Rumsfeld testily retorted that the WMDs would be found because "we know where they are."

As events unfolded dramatically in the south, the so-called northern front was strangely quiet. In the weeks prior to the war, Saddam had ordered his army units out of their bases and into freshly dug trenches. When Anmar and I had ventured north to Mosul in January, I had been astonished to see all of the defensive positions were manned but without any attempt to camouflage them. When I had suggested to Anmar that U.S. and British air superiority would slaughter the soldiers stationed here, he quickly agreed. "But if they are in the trenches, then they have no choice but to fight," he explained. "If they were in the cities, they would simply take off their uniforms and escape to their homes. That would be more embarrassing for Saddam than to have them massacred in the front lines."

It quickly became evident that Saddam's intentions would not be realized. When they received word that U.S. troops had begun securing the Baghdad airport and making probing attacks into the capital, the Iraqi soldiers on the northern front began slipping away from their bunkers.

On April 6, when U.S. Special Forces allied with Kurdish peshmerga began to attack south towards Kirkuk they met very little resistance from Saddam's forces. Their inability to find Iraqi armoured units puzzled U.S. Special Forces Sergeant Fred Walker, whose unit operated with a peshmerga detachment. "Our guys knocked out 12 Iraqi tanks with hand-held missiles, but we sure as hell didn't kill them all," Sgt. Walker told me. "Hell, there was supposed to be an entire armoured division here that's just up and gone. It sure is one hell of a mystery."

The Patriotic Union of Kurdistan's (PUK) peshmerga advanced quickly and took control of the village of Chemchemal on the outskirts of Kirkuk without a fight. The Iraqi army had already withdrawn from the area. At this point in the war, the Turkish government once again warned that Kirkuk was not to fall into the hands of the Kurdish warlords.

However, just 48 hours later Saddam's regime had collapsed in Baghdad. As if on cue, all organized resistance simply ceased and only handfuls of Fedayeen Saddam fought on. The Iraqi President himself was alleged to have fled towards Tikrit, his hometown stronghold. The U.S. media had already declared Saddam "toppled"—just like the statue in Firdos Square that was pulled down live on CNN. The Iraqi army in Kirkuk also disappeared on the night of April 8 and Kurdish peshmerga quickly moved forward past their abandoned trenches.

Surprisingly, given the warnings issued by Turkey and the concerns of the Iraqi Turkmen, the Kurds were allowed to proceed into Kirkuk without U.S. supervision. For two days, the peshmerga of both the KDP and PUK began a systematic plundering of the abandoned government offices. "They began immediately to burn all of the land deeds and birth registries," said Mustafa Kemal, the director of the ITF in Kirkuk. "Their objective was to destroy the records so that they could support their claim that Kirkuk is a Kurdish city. Without paperwork, there would be no proof of post-war ownership. The peshmerga did not limit their looting to Saddam's institutions, however, and when they stormed into a Turkmen suburb a bitter clash erupted. "In the fighting, our young men managed to force the Kurds back, but we had 10 killed and 30 wounded," said Kemal. The first Americans entered Kirkuk on April 11 and order was gradually restored.

Although the war was declared over by George W. Bush and the American occupation had begun, the Turkmen of Iraq were faced with yet another challenge: Surviving the violent peace that followed.

TOP: *U.S. soldiers in northern Iraq.* (U.S. ARMY) **ABOVE LEFT:** *Kurdish peshmerga.* **ABOVE:** *Coalition troops show solidarity before the intervention.* (U.S. DOD) **LEFT:** *Author Scott Taylor (left) with Dr. Sanan Aga and Laci Zoldi.* (SCOTT TAYLOR)

ABOVE: *American soldiers eventually began arresting Iraqi looters, but by that time virtually everything worth taking had either been stolen or destroyed.*
(BENJAMIN LOWY/CORBIS FOR TIME MAGAZINE)

OPPOSITE PAGE: *The abandoned litter of Iraq's armoured forces.* (S. TAYLOR)

Chapter Seven
Regime Removed

THE TOPPLING OF SADDAM'S STATUE on April 9, 2003 created a fall sense of achievement and caused the U.S. media to issue premature declarations of total victory in Iraq. Fedayeen fighters and even some units of the Republican Guard continued to fight rearguard actions as they retreated towards Tikrit to make their last stand. Saddam's hometown was not declared secure by coalition troops until April 28. Only 72 hours later, U.S. President George W. Bush gave his "mission accomplished" speech aboard the aircraft carrier USS *Abraham Lincoln*.

Although the American Commander-in-Chief declared an "end to combat operations in Iraq," the Iraqi resistance did not abide by his assertion. With the collapse of Saddam's Baathist regime and its security forces, the citizens of Iraq went on a massive looting spree. As U.S. Secretary of Defense Donald Rumsfeld had overruled the advice of his top generals and conducted the Iraq campaign with just 120,000 troops—not the recommended 275,000—the coalition forces were much too thin on the ground. The technological superiority of the American military made the destruction of Saddam's ill-equipped army very easy, but to replace the disbanded Iraqi police and military in the streets required far more personnel and would expose U.S. soldiers to far greater risks. As a result, Rumsfeld did nothing to inhibit the looting and quipped to reporters that the Iraqi thieves were simply "enjoying their freedom." With all government functions suspended, utilities shut down, and occupation troops unable to intervene, Iraq descended into a state of anarchy.

In some places, like Fallujah, Iraqi resistance fighters began collecting abandoned military hardware and attacking American patrols. For the most part, however, in the first weeks after Saddam's regime had collapsed, the fighting was largely conducted between roving bands of *schroogs* (thieves) and civilians trying to protect their property.

As violence continued to spread through Iraq, it became increasingly difficult for the Bush administration to justify its intervention to the world. Its claim that the mission had been accomplished seemed to be contradicted by the facts that no weapons of mass destruction (WMD) had been located and that the Iraqi dictator was still eluding capture.

Almost immediately, the White House and Pentagon began to change their spin on the reasons why the war had been waged. The focus had shifted from the possession of WMDs to the discovery of mass graves by U.S. troops. Given the media hype on this new twist, one could be forgiven for beginning to believe that George Bush had gone to war to prevent Saddam from committing genocide against his own people.

The first revelation of an alleged slaughter came during the initial week of fighting. In a warehouse outside of Basra, American troops found 400 corpses, the decomposed bodies filmed by embedded journalists. Brigadier General Vince Brooks, the U.S. military spokesman in Qatar, briefed the international press corps on the discovery. During his dramatic presentation, Brooks made a point of telling reporters that "many of the dead had been... executed" and that the site had since been sealed as it was a "possible war crime."

What Brooks neglected to clarify was *which* war. The U.S. authorities already knew that these were the corpses of Iraqi soldiers that had been killed during the Iran-Iraq conflict nearly 20 years earlier. The bodies had been stored in the Basra warehouse—tagged and identified by the International Committee of the Red Cross (ICRC)—as part of ongoing efforts to repatriate Iraqi war dead. Similarly, many of the other mass graves discovered by the U.S. military and reported to the media were those of Shiia, Kurdish and Turkmen rebels, killed during the 1991 post-Gulf War uprising.

While there was no denying that Saddam's security forces had exacted a brutal revenge on those involved in the revolution, at the time of the killings some 500,000 U.S. coalition troops were still based in the Persian Gulf and allied aircraft were routinely flying overhead on patrol. When an international intervention could have easily been mounted against Saddam to save the lives of the rebels, America had turned its back on them.

Without probing questions by the media, the U.S. State Department was now using these deaths as justification for its invasion of Iraq. To perpetuate this myth, senior spokespersons reiterated the genocide spin as often as possible. Before he was replaced as interim governor in May 2003—after just five months as the U.S. civil administrator in charge of reconstruction and humanitarian aid in post-war Iraq—Jay Garner told the media that "up to one million bodies" would be found buried in Saddam's mass graves. U.S. Vice President Dick Cheney added to the chorus by proclaiming that regardless of whether or not WMDs are ever found, had the U.S. not intervened when it did "the torture chambers would still be operating" and Saddam would be on target to kill his annual "10,000 innocent civilians."

Of course, it was difficult to explain why occupation troops were being attacked if the Bush's coalition of the willing had indeed just saved the Iraqi people from a genocidal maniac. To further convince the American public that some Iraqis were greeting U.S. troops as 'liberators,' Interim Governor Jay Garner went so far as to stage a victory parade through the streets of Sulaimaniyah. Still eager to curry U.S. favour, Jalal Talabani and his PUK supporters willingly complied with the governor's request. Thousands of Kurds lined the streets to wave flags and throw flowers at Garner as he walked along shaking hands and smiling to the crowds. It was a wonderful photo op, and not a single U.S. reporter noted that the flag they were waving was not Iraqi, but had the distinctive sunburst pattern of the Kurdish nationalist party. Nor was it mentioned that Sulaimaniyah had not been under Saddam's control since 1991, when the region had been 'liberated' by Kurdish peshmerga—not U.S. troops in 2003. As the three northern provinces remained under tight Kurdish control, the U.S. occupational force considered them as 'stable' and therefore they required only minimal military presence.

Despite the apparent calm in the region, below the surface

inter-factional rivalry had started to simmer. Thousands of Kurds clogged the roads as they headed south into Mosul and Kirkuk. The Americans simply saw this as a reversal of Saddam's Arabification policy and thought that these people were heading home to reclaim their lost property. In some cases this was true. But with the great effort taken by the peshmerga to eradicate all registration and land deeds, a much more sinister program of ethnic cleansing was underway.

"If they can flood the area with enough Kurdish settlers prior to a census then they will be able to substantiate their claims that Kirkuk is a Kurdish city," said Mustafa Kemal, the director of the ITF office. "At the same time, because the Kurds control the borders, they are preventing Turkmen exiles from returning home."

During my first post-war trip back into Iraq, I witnessed this first hand.

~~~~~~~~~~

Only days before the war began, two Mukhabarat officers paid me an official visit at my hotel in Baghdad. Although it had been my intention to remain in Iraq and report on the war for the duration, the secret service agents advised me that this was no longer possible. When I asked them why, they replied in a sinister tone, "Because you are a Mossad spy!" Apparently, a competing journalist had told them this. Although there was no evidence to support this ridiculous claim, with a U.S. invasion imminent Iraq's intelligence agency was taking no chances. My expulsion was subsequently well publicized and the Iraqi authorities even received a stern rebuke from the Association of Foreign Journalists.

I was suddenly a spectator without a vantage point. Although several hundred foreign journalists had been allowed pre-war passage and issued credentials at Massif Salahudin, I had missed the window of opportunity. In an effort to regain entry prior to the start of the war, I attempted to cross back into Iraq through the Turkish border and into the Kurd-controlled territory. But the Turks kept the border tightly shut, and I had to resign myself to the fact that I would be watching most of the U.S.-led intervention on television from the Turkish village of Silopi.

At this point, Sasha Uzunov, an Australian soldier-turned-photojournalist I have known for years, linked up with me in Silopi. Hoping that a less-travelled side road might offer access to the border, Sasha and I had rented bicycles from a couple of local Kurdish teenagers and attempted to cross the frontier. However, after a 42-kilometre miserably cold trek through freshly ploughed fields we were deterred by red triangular signs warning of minefields. Reluctantly, we returned to Silopi. With the advent of war and events unfolding at such a rapid pace, there were no signs that the Turks would reopen the border any time soon so I decided to head for home.

Travelling back through this same territory in southern Turkey a little more than a month later was almost a surreal experience. A land that had then been bustling with wartime activity had returned just as quickly to being a sleepy little corner of the world. All of the American transport aircraft and freight containers, which were never officially authorized to be there in the first place, that I had seen on my last trip, had since left the Diyarbakir airport. Although the U.S. troops had gone, Turkey's 7th Armoured Corps remained bivouacked in the area, but its state of alert had been greatly reduced. These soldiers now lounged in the sun or played football while most of the armoured vehicles were covered by tarps. Prior to the war, this border crossing had been a virtual "rolling pipeline" as tankers delivered oil exports out of Iraq. Now, this border was still officially closed and thousands of oil trucks sat idle in parked columns stretching back some 30 kilometres from the crossing point.

It was still difficult to enter Iraq at that time and the Iraqi Turkmen Front in Ankara helped to arrange a special clearance for me. It had taken several days to process, but in the end the Turkish General Staff allowed me to accompany a few returning expatriate Iraqi Turkmen as a 'tourist.' On the Turkish side of the border I met with Muaffaq Hacioglu, the ITF representative responsible for all transit arrangements. Tall, thin and sporting an oversized Ottoman-style moustache, Muaffaq spoke little English but was genuinely friendly. As a resident of Zakho, located just inside the Iraqi boundary, Muaffaq had earned himself a well-deserved popularity as goalie on the local football team. In all, there were about a dozen of us making the crossing that day and our group formed a small convoy of vehicles. Muaffaq had arranged our exit visas and cleared us through Turkish MIT (intelligence).

Once we had crossed the border and were on the Kurdish side I was surprised to see that there was no U.S. military presence, only peshmerga belonging to Massoud Barzani's KDP. Given the animosity between the two ethnic groups, I found it odd that an ITF representative like Muaffaq could have facilitated our passage. I quickly realized that passage through this border crossing presented a perfect opportunity for Barzani's ruling faction—and a very lucrative one at that.

While the KDP's Asaish recorded and searched everyone

entering "Iraqi Kurdistan," Barzani's "customs officials" were free to levy their own entry taxes. For an individual visa, the cost was $50 US, which amounts to a princely sum in a country where policemen often made only $10 a month. However the real money-maker for the KDP was the amount of "duty" that was assigned to imported goods, which seemed to be predicated upon one's ability to pay. "Welcome to the new liberated Iraq," said Ahmet Hosad, a 24-year-old Iraqi Turkmen who worked as one of Muaffaq's drivers. "We are now free to charge and be charged for just about anything."

One of my Turkmen travel companions was Zygon Chechen. A resident of Kirkuk, Chechen had fled to Toronto after the collapse of the 1991 uprising. When he had left Iraq twelve years before, he had been robbed at gunpoint by peshmerga. This time, it was at the hands of Barzani's customs officers. Chechen had purchased a used Opel station wagon in Germany for $3,000 US. He and his nephew had then driven the vehicle to the Iraqi border with the intention of visiting relatives in Kirkuk and Erbil. After hours of negotiations, the Kurds levied a $1,600 US tariff on his vehicle and possessions. After Chechen paid the fine he was left with exactly $22 US in his pocket. With no means of getting funds to replace the money or even the ability to use credit cards while in Iraq, that money would have to last Chechen for the duration of two-week visit. "Not exactly a grateful welcome home for an old soldier is it?" asked Chechen.

I got to know that 'old soldier' quite well over the next five hours. Since the rest of the Turkmen delegation had already departed, Chechen's vehicle was my last hope for a ride to Kirkuk. I agreed to pay him $20 US for gas and buy them both lunch in exchange for a lift. The only problem was fitting me in the car as the Opel had been overloaded to the point where you could not see out of the rear-window. For an ex-soldier, Zygon Chechen is of considerable girth, possibly tipping the scales around 300 lbs while his nephew has a slender build. Although I am tall and lean, I could not manage to squeeze in between the car's small bucket seats. In the end, we placed a small cooler between the two seats; by straddling it and lifting my head and shoulders out through the sunroof of the car, I was able to cram myself between the two Chechens. In the 40-degree heat, however, this was decidedly uncomfortable, not to mention very dangerous. "No police, no problem!" shouted the robust Chechen. Speed, however, was also a problem as it became difficult to breathe when going faster than 60 km an hour. But we had struck a deal: Chechen needed the money and I needed the ride. So we plodded onward to Kirkuk.

Because we could not travel at top speed and with the delay at the border, we did not arrive until well after dark. With the electricity not yet restored, Kirkuk was pitch black on this hot summer night. Shadowy figures could barely be seen moving along narrow alleyways and we could hear the rattling of occasional gunfire. The worst part of all was that, within minutes of entering the city, Chechen was hopelessly lost. He had not been back in the past 12 years and had quickly become disoriented in the darkness. At one intersection a number of armed men had demanded that we stop. One of them started to approach our car with his Kalashnikov pointed at the windshield. Chechen's alarm quickly turned to glee. "Ahmet! Ahmet! You are a fucker of goats!" he yelled in Turkish. Translating his greeting to me, Chechen explained happily that Ahmet was his cousin. After years of exile, Zygon Chechen was finally home—and among friends.

When I learned that this armed detachment was a security force from the Iraqi Turkmen Front, I realized that I had successfully reached my destination. I was informed that Mustafa Kemal and Dr. Mustafa Ziya were expecting me and that I should meet with them in the morning. I was then taken to a nearby hotel. The place was filthy; there were stains on the rugs, fleas in the bed, and I found a four-inch cockroach in the shower stall. On the plus side, it did have a generator but the air conditioner was broken. Nearby, on the darkened city streets, the shouts of looters were occasionally punctuated by bursts of gunfire. For $6 US a night—including breakfast—I figured I couldn't complain.

THE NEXT MORNING, I ate an early breakfast of boiled eggs, flatbread and tea al fresco. From my table, I could see that a long queue of angry drivers waited at a nearby petrol station. A small patrol of U.S. troops were present, but the female military police officer in charge was unable to cope with the waiting motorists' rising tempers. And without a translator, the soldiers could not communicate. Shortly after the pumps opened at 7:00 a.m., a fist fight broke out between the gas station attendant and an angry customer. Shouts and punches flew. The angry mob of fed up drivers physically manhandled the abusive man to the roadside. Almost hysterical at being expelled from the queue, Sezqin Mirkhan pleaded his case with the American soldiers. "I have been waiting in line for four days and now they say they won't serve me because I'm a Kurdish *schroog* (thief)," said Mirkhan. "Please do something to help me."

Specialist Amy Johnson, the young military policewoman Mirkhan had asked to intervene on his behalf, appeared both

TOP: *U.S. soldiers try to police the queue for gasoline in post-war Kirkuk.* (SCOTT TAYLOR) **ABOVE:** *Iraqis on patrol with American soldiers appear more like prisoners than allies.* (SCOTT TAYLOR)

TOP: Turkey-Iraq border crossing at Silopi. Of note are the stolen cars that are seen being transported into Iraq as oil tanker trucks exit. *(SCOTT TAYLOR)* ***ABOVE:*** Photojournalist Sasha Uzunov as a soldier with the Australian Army in East Timor. *(COURTESY SASHA UZUNOV)*

exasperated and a little frightened at the events unfolding around her. "We can't help you, this is an internal problem," Johnson told him. "We are here only to provide security and we don't have enough people to help you." The Kurdish driver was led away from the pumps without any gasoline.

Ahmet, a Turkmen waiter at the hotel, approached my table. "Do not feel any pity for that man," he said. "He is a *schroog*. We know who is from Kirkuk, and which of these Kurds came after the war to steal from us. Unfortunately, to the Americans all Iraqis look the same."

The shortage of gasoline across the country was a new phenomenon for Iraqis and while some post-war confusion was to be expected, the failure of the U.S. authorities to ensure adequate distribution had caused tensions to mount. After my breakfast, I walked to the nearby gas station and along the line-up to discover that it stretched back nearly six kilometres. Because I looked like an American, I was heckled in Arabic, Kurdish and Turkish by many of the frustrated drivers.

Near the end of the line, things became much more tense when a giant of a man blocked my passage. In fluent English he demanded, "Where the fuck is our gas? What have you Americans done with all of Iraq's oil?" Before I could respond, the waiting drivers began to gather round and started yelling at me in a variety of languages. Before the situation could turn violent, a passing U.S. Special Forces patrol braked to a halt to investigate the commotion. The .50 calibre machine gun mounted on top of the vehicle proved enough of a threat to disperse the mob.

Staff Sergeant Al Tifton offered me a lift and asked me what had caused all the fuss. When I explained the situation, Tifton laughed and said, "We've got plenty of gas up at our air base.

Hell, we'll probably have to start drinking the stuff now that we've run out of places to put it."

~~~~~~~~~~

For all those American pundits that claimed the intervention in Iraq was "not about oil," the reality on the ground appeared to be quite a bit different. While the U.S. troops deployed in northern Iraq were admittedly thinly stretched, there was no shortage of troops available to secure facilities related to Iraq's oil infrastructure. In fact, the first large detachment of U.S. personnel I encountered was patrolling the grounds of the North Oil Company. Three squads of soldiers—all members of the 173rd Airborne Brigade—were mounted in armoured Hummers. Squeezed in beside them were a few local police officers. Clad in dark green uniforms and armed only with Billy clubs, the Iraqis looked more like prisoners than police-men as they sat next to the paratroopers in their flak jackets, helmets and visors.

The 173rd Airborne patrol had been curious to see me out on my own taking photographs, and had roared up beside me to demand identification. Once they had looked over my press pass, they relaxed and became eager to chat. When I asked about the Iraqis accompanying them, Staff Sergeant Sanders, a big paratrooper from Texas, drawled, "We wanted to put some locals back on the streets 'cause we didn't have a clue what was going on when we first got here." When I asked how they had selected the individuals to serve as police, he didn't hesitate. "Since it seemed that Kurds was doing most of the looting, we figured it was a smart bet to hire Arabs to keep them in line." When I asked him why they didn't consider hiring some Turkmen, Sanders scratched his head and look puzzled. "What the fuck is a Turkmen?" From behind him in the Hummer, one of the Iraqi policemen who had overheard our conversation yelled back, "I'm a Turkmen."

More than a month into the occupation of Kirkuk, the U.S. troops were still just beginning to understand the diverse cultural composition of the city. Lowering his voice to a barely audible whisper, Sanders said, "I thought that he was an Arab because he wasn't a Kurd. And now you tell me that there are Turkmen people here too?" As I started to explain to him that Chaldean Christians, Assyrians and Yazidi also lived in this area, his eyes began to glaze over and he held up his hand for me to stop. "I never was much good at geography," he said.

LATER THAT MORNING, I walked a short distance from my hotel to the central office of the Iraqi Turkmen Front. Across the street from this building, a small house flew the distinctive blue and white flag of the ITF. While the larger building was used primarily for administration, I learned that the second one was being converted into a fortified stronghold, and saw a number of armed ITF volunteers milling about in the courtyard.

Until now, very few foreign journalists had come to Kirkuk, and my arrival at the ITF office had caused some initial concern. Although several men were in the office, none of them spoke English. And although they understood that I was looking for Mustafa Kemal and Mustafa Ziya, they could not answer my questions. Through hand gestures, I was offered a seat and a cup of chai (Iraqi tea) until a translator could be found. Several minutes later I was greeted by Aydin Aslin, a towering Turkmen with white hair and a broad smile. In excellent English Aslin explained to me that this bureau was only one of many the organization had in Kirkuk. "When Saddam's regime collapsed, everybody rushed out to lay claim to former federal buildings," he said. "The ITF managed to secure several of these properties."

Although he was on his way to work, Aslin nevertheless offered to drive me to the ITF's main headquarters. As we pulled out onto the main street, I saw that yet another brawl had erupted in the gasoline queue. "You have to forgive them—it is a new experience for Iraqis to have to wait for fuel. Saddam used to subsidize petrol, and there was always plenty of it," explained the big Turkmen. "Under the U.S. occupation, the price has quadrupled (from 6 cents to 24 cents per litre) and selling black market gas has become an overnight industry."

As we drove, Aslin explained that he had returned to his position as the chief oil advisor at the Kirkuk-based North Oil Company at the request of the Americans. "I only missed two days of work as a result of the war," said Aslin. "As soon as the North Oil Company was in U.S. military hands, they came to my house to invite me back to work. They said their number one priority was to get the oil flowing again."

When I asked how a Turkmen had managed to achieve such a senior position in the North Oil Company during the Baath regime, Aslin replied: "They were not complete idiots. As I was a capable engineer, they gave me some responsibility—and then my Baath party superiors would take the credit." Admitting that he had been forced to take out a membership in the Baath party, he added, "But I was never involved in politics. I was simply concerned with keeping the decrepit oil industry's infrastructure from shutting down completely."

The newly acquired ITF headquarters was quite a large, stand-alone complex, built around a central courtyard and which can be easily defended. At 6 feet 5 inches, Aslin is easily identifiable and well known among the Turkmen citizens of Kirkuk, and the ITF militia guards had not bothered to ask for identification and just ushered us through the gates. Upon entering the building, we were greeted by Mustafa Ziya, and I was soon introduced to Mustafa Kemal. Arrangements had been made for me to interview them in an upstairs boardroom.

Seeing my interest in the armed guards posted at all the windows, Kemal explained, "We have to protect ourselves." When I asked him what the strength of the ITF militia was, Kemal claimed that "There are only about 200 full-time volunteers, but all Turkmen males have taken military training as conscripts and most households have hidden weapons. If the Kurds push us then we can mobilize thousands of Turkmen to defend ourselves."

As we would soon find out, the Kurds were out to pressure the ITF, but they did not act alone. Hearing a commotion in a lower hallway, we were interrupted by an anxious guard. "The Americans are raiding the building!" he shouted.

As we came down the main staircase, I saw an American officer in the middle of the courtyard, directing a platoon of heavily armed police to search the adjoining offices. Although the Turkmen militiamen allowed the U.S. troops to entry the compound, the situation was very tense. Kemal and Ziya asked the U.S. major for an explanation, but he instead focused his attention on me. When he saw me take photographs of the American soldiers, the startled officer snapped rudely, "Who the fuck are you?" I responded by bluffing that I was someone in authority: "Major, I believe the question is, who the fuck are you? And what are you doing searching these premises?" The bluff worked, and the American soldier began explaining that informants had advised them that the building was being used for "anti-coalition activities."

Within a few minutes Mustafa Kemal was able to prove that the ITF was properly registered with the Coalition Provisional Authority (CPA) and that his guards had been authorized to carry weapons by none other than the U.S. commander himself. With the paperwork in order, the search was called off and everyone relaxed. The major revealed that the allegations had been made by a local Kurdish commander in the PUK peshmerga, someone the Americans had mistakenly trusted as an ally. It seemed clear that the Kurds' intent had been to provoke the Turkmen militia into an exchange of gunfire with the much heavier armed Americans. This would have resulted in a bloodbath and the arrest of the ITF's senior leaders. "This was a dirty trick, and we were lucky that our men showed restraint," said Kemal.

~~~~~~~~~~

The cat and mouse games between the Kurds and Turkmen would continue, but Jalal Talabani's PUK was soon able to established virtual control over Kirkuk. Although the CPA had brought in a number of Kurdish policemen from Erbil and Sulaimaniyah to patrol the streets and monitor traffic, any action against insurgents was only undertaken by the U.S. 173rd Airborne Brigade. While both of these forces maintained their own separate checkpoints and patrols, the third level of authority established in Kirkuk was that of Talabani's peshmerga. Independent of the CPA or any U.S. command, the armed

Kurdish militiamen were free to stop and search civilian cars. In September 2003, when I had returned to Kirkuk in the company of Laci Zoldi, my Hungarian colleague, we discovered for ourselves the level of control the PUK exercised in Kirkuk.

Laci and I had originally gone to the large, heavily guarded PUK headquarters in Kirkuk to ask about the possibility of interviewing Jalal Talabani in his office in Sulaimaniyah. Telephone systems being unreliable, we had hoped to have a definite appointment before undertaking the two-hour drive from Kirkuk. We presumed that the local commander would at least be able to put us in touch with Talabani's aides. However, there appeared to be some confusion as to our request and we were told to come back the following morning for a personal audience with Jalal Jawhar Azzez, the "Governor of Kirkuk."

Our curiosity somewhat piqued, we returned the next day at the allotted time and were ushered into a large waiting room where a number of Kurdish civilians were already seated. Servants brought us each a tea. All those assembled seemed apprehensive about their imminent audience with Azzez.

Eventually the elegant, grey-haired, self-appointed Governor of Kirkuk entered from a side room and took up position behind his desk like a judge presiding over a courtroom. As we watched the first few Kurdish presentations, it became clear that Azzez and the PUK were as powerful in this region as any feudal lord. The former peshmerga colonel and cousin to Jalal Talabani resolved such issues as trivial as business disputes and marriage arrangements. After hearing brief submissions, Azzez would pass judgment with the wave of a hand and a few words to his clerk who dutifully recorded the proceedings. Without a word of rebuttal or challenge, the plaintiffs and defendants alike were then escorted from the room by peshmerga guards.

With the crowd having thinned, when Azzez looked up he had taken note of Laci and me, and he issued a flurry of questions. A Kurdish translator, Hal Gurd, approached us. "Are you the journalists who were requesting a highway pass to Sulaimaniyah?" Gurd asked. While we noted that Azzez was also in the business of selling passage on what were ostensibly free roads, we hurriedly clarified our request. Again, the translation left much to be desired and soon Azzez thought that we wanted to interview him. Obviously flattered that foreign media would have sought him out for comment, he clapped his hands to adjourn the proceedings and invited us into his private chambers.

Throughout the course of our interview, Azzez maintained the PUK party line that the Kurds wished only to operate within a central Iraqi federation. When I asked him why the flag of Kurdistan flew over the building, he became visibly nervous. "That will be replaced tomorrow," he assured us.

Earlier that month, U.S. Ambassador and Administrator of the Coalition Provisional Authority Paul Bremer had instructed the removal of all partisan flags from public buildings in northern Iraq. When the demand had not been met, an American patrol had attempted to forcibly carry out the order in the city of Sulaimaniyah. In response, a mob of Kurds attacked the U.S. soldiers, rolled their Hummers over and set them ablaze. The soldiers wisely beat on a hasty retreat. This incident had gone largely unreported in the media, but it had badly shaken Bremer's relationship with the PUK and, obviously, Governor Azzez did not want to reignite the issue in Kirkuk.

My main purpose for this visit to Kirkuk had been to attend the Iraqi Turkmen Front's leadership conference. Following the collapse of Saddam's regime, ITF insiders knew that in order to keep the movement alive ITF President Dr. Sanan Aga had brokered an agreement with the former regime. Although such co-operation should not be judged in hindsight, it was now considered a detrimental legacy for the ITF, and Sanan Aga had agreed to step down as President of the ITF.

There had been a lot of fanfare in the Iraqi Turkmen community over the upcoming convention, and many expatriates had been invited to participate. A number of Turkish journalists from Ankara also accepted invitations to attend if for no other reason than to enter the post-war chaos that was Iraq in a relatively secure, escorted column. As things turned out, the only international media in attendance at the conference were Laci Zoldi and me.

As hundreds of delegates merged into the conference centre, it was readily apparent that the local U.S. commander was taking no chances if factional violence erupted. Squads of paratroopers patrolled from nearby rooftops and all roads leading to the centre were closed to the public. In recognition of the U.S. contribution, Colonel Mayville of the 173rd Airborne Brigade, the senior U.S. officer in Kirkuk, was invited to make a presentation at the ITF convention. Although Mayville spoke at length about Iraq embarking on "the peaceful road to a real democracy," he failed to appreciate some of the political machinations that were taking place at this very event. Many of those present were not Turkmen, but tribal leaders of Kirkuk's multiethnic Arab community. On the first morning of the conference, each took to the stage to express their allegiance and solidarity with their "Turkmen brothers" in the event of "emergency circumstances." In essence they were brokering a military alliance with the Turkmen against any aggression by Kurdish peshmerga.

In recognition of my writings about the issues affecting the Iraqi Turkmen, I was called to the podium to receive a plaque. Asif Sertturkmen, the Canadian ITF representative, made the presentation. Although few in the audience could speak English, I wished the Turkmen success in their "peaceful process towards democratically electing their own leader." The translated version of my comments drew applause, but unbeknownst to those inside the hall, the ITF convention was experiencing some difficulties. In an effort to sway the vote, forged entry passes had been issued and the number of registered delegates soon outnumbered the hall's seating capacity.

When security guards tried to seal the entrance, a woman began screaming hysterically that she was being denied her rights. When a fat man echoed this sentiment, one of the guards jumped onto the barricade beside him and started punching him in the face. The crowd went berserk as the blood and punches flew. The clamour attracted Turkish cameramen who rushed to the scene only to find themselves roughed up by some ITF guards. When order was finally restored, angry delegates shouted insults and the Turkish media threatened to boycott the remainder of the conference. The situation was only defused when Dr. Mustafa Ziya addressed the crowd and pleaded for forgiveness. "The Iraqi people have never before tasted democracy," he said, "so it is only natural that they don't yet fully understand the process."

Somewhat placated, the Turkish media agreed to return to the convention hall. Further proof that the concept of a democratic process was not yet understood came that night when journalists were offered "exclusive interviews with the new president"—before the votes had even been cast. As predicted by his handlers, Dr. Faruk Abdullah Abdurrahman proved to be the winning candidate. In his victory speech, Abdurrahman pledged to lead the Turkmen "into a new era for Iraq."

The only question was, would he survive long enough to keep his promise?

ABOVE: *The vandalized remnants of Saddam's many statues can be seen throughout Iraq and are a constant reminder that the U.S. achieved only a "regime removal" and not a regime change.* (SCOTT TAYLOR)

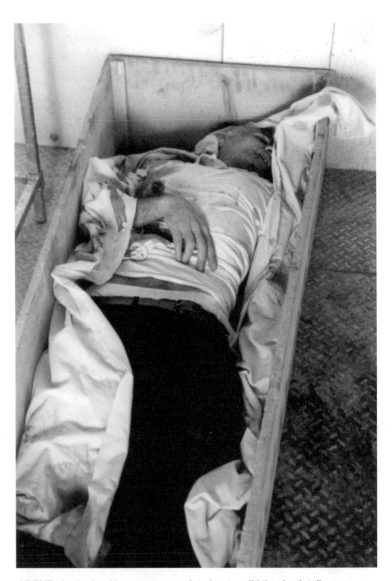

ABOVE: *As the Iraqi insurgency escalated so too did the death toll among civilians. This man was killed in Sadr City, an impoverished suburb of Baghdad, during fighting on April 5, 2004. (SCOTT TAYLOR)*
OPPOSITE PAGE: *The Iraqi Turkmen Front headquarters in Kirkuk. (S. TAYLOR)*

Chapter Eight
The Way Ahead

ON NOVEMBER 21, 2003, shortly after 10:00 a.m., a tremendous blast detonated outside the PUK headquarters of "Governor" Jalal Jawhar Azzez in Kirkuk. Estimated to contain no less that one ton of nitroglycerine, the car bomb had shattered the eight-foot long garden wall and totally destroyed Azzez's office suite—the same rooms were where Laci Zoldi and I had chatted with Azzez. Chunks of twisted granite and burnt furniture now littered the street. Three peshmerga guards that were patrolling the garden were killed instantly in the blast. Azzez, who was not in his office at the time of the attack, believed he was the intended target.

When I arrived on the scene the following day, I was greeted cordially by Hal Gurd, the senior Asaish officer who had acted as translator during my interview with Azzez. The 57-year-old was a big, burly man with the flattened nose of a boxer. "He looks like he's killed many people and enjoyed the experience," Laci had told me after our first meeting with Gurd. It was an apt description. While he smiled often enough, Gurd's eyes held a steely gaze that could be quite unnerving.

On this day, however, Gurd wore sunglasses and appeared to be visibly shaken up by the bombing. As he showed us the extent of the devastation, Gurd stated out that his agents were in the process of examining the remains of the car. All the evidence and clues that were found had been collected and piled in the garden next to PUK office. Workmen were already in the process of rebuilding the protective outer wall, while scores of armed peshmerga provided security from the rooftop and adjacent bunkers. Hal Gurd spent a few minutes combing through the collected auto parts before he discovered what he had been looking for. The grisly object he held up was a couple of vertebrae held together by some burnt skin and muscle. A small patch of cloth embedded in the skin appeared to be that of a red and white headscarf.

"They want us to believe that this was the work of suicide bomber, and that is why they put an Arab's body in the car," said Gurd. "However, the remains of the remotely controlled detonator would suggest that this man didn't know the purpose of the mission." When asked who he thought had tried to assassinate Jawal Azzez, Gurd did not hesitate to reply, "Turkish intelligence."

Although he could offer no direct proof to support his allegations, Gurd said his agents would continue to investigate the car bombing based on this assumption. "The Americans announced that this was the work of al-Qaeda Islamic fundamentalists, but they did not even approach the bomb site," he said. "In fact, they still believe that the U.S. headquarters [just 500 metres away] was the intended target, and that the bomb detonated prematurely."

The Americans in Kirkuk had good reason to feel threatened. Although the stiffening resistance was gaining momentum in the central "Sunni Triangle" of Iraq, it had yet to spread north. But anti-occupation violence was on the increase. A major incident had been the September 10, 2003 bombing of a U.S. "safe house" in the city of Erbil. It was estimated that nearly eight tons of explosives packed into a truck had caused the devastating blast. While several CIA and Mossad intelligence agents inside the house at the time of the explosion were killed, the destruction had not been limited to the target. When the dust settled and the bodies were counted, it was believed that three Iraqi civilians, including a two-year-old boy, were dead and another 55 wounded. The combined U.S.-Israeli intelligence casualties were never revealed but estimated to number more than two dozen. It had been a well planned and carefully executed strike.

Attacks against American soldiers in northern Iraq were now becoming commonplace. In November 2003, resistance fighters had riddled an SUV driven by two U.S. Special Forces soldiers. After bringing the vehicle to a halt, the Iraqi fighters pulled the wounded soldiers from the vehicle and slit their throats. Crowds of onlookers cheered and danced at the spectacle.

"We are certainly not being greeted as liberators," my old friend Eddie Calis told me when I met up with him in Kirkuk later that same day. Calis is a Palestinian-American and he was deployed to Iraq as a civilian security advisor at the Kirkuk airfield. When U.S. forces began launching major counteroffensives against the resistance fighters in hotbeds such as Fallujah, many of the guerrillas headed north to find softer targets. The Kirkuk airfield was soon coming under almost nightly mortar attacks.

"As a demonstration of U.S. determination, we have begun firing our own mortars in return," said Calis. When I asked him just what the hell they would fire at, he smiled and said, "Would you believe an empty field? ... We want to be certain that we don't create any more collateral damage among the Kirkuk citizens. Our blasting away is to bolster the morale of the local population into thinking that it's a two-way fight. The truth is, we don't have a clue where the terrorists are."

As the U.S. troops in the north came under increased attacks, the various Iraqi factions stepped up their own turf wars. On February 1, 2004, Massoud Barzani's Kurdistan Democratic Party and Jalal Talabani's Patriotic Union of Kurdistan were simultaneously attacked. At two separate KDP events in Erbil, suicide bombers had gained entry into the crowded gardens where receptions were taking place. As security at both functions was tight, it was believed that the assailants had been allowed to enter with the compliance of treacherous peshmerga guards. The results were terrifying and brutal. An estimated 65 Kurds were killed and another 200 wounded in the blast, making it the bloodiest attack until then in post-war Iraq. Many of the casualties were members of Barzani's clan as well as senior leaders of Talabani's PUK.

Driving through Erbil the next night, I learned first hand just how edgy and vengeful the Kurdish peshmerga had become in the wake of the bombings. After our car was halted at a KDP checkpoint, about a half dozen peshmerga emerged from the gloom to surround us. With a Kalashnikov pointed at the driver's head, the Kurds demanded to know if there were any Arabs in the car. One of my travelling companions joked, "What about a Canadian?" In response we heard the distinctive metallic click as the peshmerga cocked his assault rifle. The Kurds were obviously in no mood to joke. Once our identification had been examined, we were waved through the checkpoint.

Driving away, we realized that the car in front of us had not been so lucky. Two male occupants were dragged from their vehicle and thrown to the ground. Several peshmerga started viciously kicking them. In the back seat, a young woman wept in fear as she tried to comfort two infants. Just past the KDP checkpoint sat an Iraqi police vehicle, but the Kurdish policemen inside it made no effort to intervene.

Once again, the official word was that the February 1 bombing had been the handiwork of the Ansar al-Islam, a Kurdish Islamic extremist group with links to al-Qaeda. But from the rounding up and beating of Arab suspects, I had to conclude that the Kurds had a different idea as to the actual culprits were. "They know the truth, but they also know that right now there is so much anger that the people cannot be told," said Mahmud, a 35-year-old Kurdish expatriate who lived in Sweden. "Otherwise the streets of Erbil will run red with the blood of Arabs."

I had met Mahmud at the Turkish border crossing and we had agreed to share a taxi to Kirkuk. He was en route to a family reunion when he learned that his brother had been one of those killed in the bombing. "My brother was a senior official in the KDP, and I assure you his death will be avenged," declared Mahmud. "I will carry on his work to ensure that his sacrifice is ultimately rewarded with the creation of an independent Kurdistan."

As we continued south from Erbil, Mahmud and I discussed

the widening division between Arabs and Kurds. Meanwhile, U.S. troops in Kirkuk were involved in yet another incident that would only serve to alienate them further from the Turkmen population. Just after 9:00 p.m. an explosion ripped through the central square. Although it was still early, the streets of Kirkuk were almost entirely deserted. A U.S. ambush patrol stationed on a rooftop had spotted a suspicious-looking vehicle near the blast site. Tracking the car with their night-vision goggles, the Americans waited until the driver was within range and then opened up with a deadly burst of machine-gun fire. A total of 53 bullets smashed into the BMW, thirteen of which penetrated the driver's head and torso.

Eyewitnesses reported that 21-year-old Sinan Ibrahim Ismail was seen moving inside his car for several minutes after the attack but that Iraqi civilians were prevented from providing medical aid by the U.S. patrol which had secured the area. "When I asked them why this happened, an American told me that 'this was a terrorist' in the car," said Dr. Ali Tirzo. "But when I looked at the vehicle I told them they were wrong; this was my cousin."

Local Iraqi police arrived at the scene and confirmed that Ismail was not the suspect the U.S. soldiers were looking for. The patrol had mistakenly shot up the wrong BMW. Far from being a member of the resistance, Ismail had been studying nursing at the local college, while working part time at the nearby U.S. air base. While Ismail's family and the Turkmen community had been outraged at his senseless death, the callousness subsequently demonstrated by the Americans only exacerbated the situation.

When U.S. authorities had made no effort to contact Ismail's family, the boy's uncle Jallil Amen approached the Americans.

Ismail's father had passed away in 1993, and as the eldest brother in the family such affairs had become Amen's responsibility. "I was told that the matter was under investigation and that I would be notified of the final decision. Three months later they telephoned my shop and told me to come to their office."

After being escorted inside the American compound, Amen was introduced to a U.S. military Judge Advocate General (JAG) captain who presented him with a letter that read: "On behalf of the coalition forces in Kirkuk, Iraq, I want to express my deep sympathy for you and your family for the loss of your son Sinan. I know that this is a difficult time for you but please know that your son was a good man and there is absolutely no evidence that he was working with the anti-coalition forces. I am sorry that we could not deliver our sentiments in person, but security risks prevent this from being possible. I sincerely hope the best for you and your family in the future." The letter was signed "Sincerely" by Samuel Schubert, Major U.S. Army Command, Judge Advocate.

To clarify Major Schubert's letter, it must be pointed out that he was stationed at the U.S. air base in Kirkuk, five kilometres from the civil administration building where the letter was delivered to Amen by a captain. Along with this single piece of correspondence emblazoned with the U.S. Department of Defense letterhead, Amen was handed ten crisp new $100 bills and a receipt to sign.

When he saw the money, Amen had been incredulous. "What is this for?" he asked the captain. "The BMW alone was with $5000!" The U.S. officer calmly explained that the U.S. does not make restitution for war-related damages. Amen was informed that the money was in fact a "grant" from the international aid fund. "He wanted me to know that the U.S. government was in no way liable for the incident and that the money I was to receive was not from the American military," said Amen. "It was offered only as a gesture of sympathy."

Although Amen can speak passable English, like many of his fellow Turkmen he can only read Arabic script. As such, he had no idea that the receipt he signed in exchange for the cash was a legal agreement whereby he waived all rights to seek further compensation from the U.S. government. "I was told that if I don't sign the receipt and take the money then I would not receive the letter. The last thing the captain told me as he handed me the $1000 was, 'Remember, we [Americans] don't put a dollar figure on a human life.' "

The Turkmen of Kirkuk were still mourning the death of Ismail when they were shocked to learn that the Americans had arrested Najmaden Kasab Uglo. A Turkmen activist, Najmaden had been one of the first expatriates to return to Iraq after Saddam's regime collapsed. Within hours of the PUK peshmerga's pushing past the abandoned Iraqi trenches, Najmaden and several armed Turkmen followers arrived in Kirkuk and began galvanizing the ITF into action. For over a year, Najmaden was able to carry on his activities without interference. However, on March 5, 2004 at around 10:00 a.m., armoured U.S. Humvees had suddenly swept in to surround the ITF offices. Acting on a tip from a Kurdish informant who had accused Najmaden of anti-American activity, a platoon of heavily armed military police stormed into the ITF compound while their comrades blocked all the outside exits.

Formerly a long-time prisoner of Saddam's Mukhabarat, Najmaden could not believe this was happening to him. "You can only imagine my shock, horror and disappointment when the Americans came and my nightmare started all over again," said the 49-year-old Turkmen. Handcuffed and dragged from the ITF office, Najmaden would spend the next 15 days locked in a prison at the nearby American airfield. His clothing and personal effects were exchanged for a bright orange jumpsuit emblazoned with the number 70, and he was herded into a large cell with 15 to 20 other "terror" suspects.

While admitting that the U.S. authorities did not subject him to torture, Najmaden conceded that the uncertainty surrounding his imprisonment was emotionally stressful. "The Americans did not tell anyone where I was, and I had no communication with the outside world. I was not charged with a specific crime and I was not appointed any legal counsel," Najmaden recalled.

Nevertheless, he felt that he was one of the luckier prisoners. "I was brought in for interrogation on three separate occasions, where it became clear to me that the Americans had no substantive evidence—only the allegation from a Kurdish informant." Many of the other prisoners would spend more than three weeks locked up without even being brought in for questioning. "I was given special status because they knew that I was a leader among the Turkmen."

While Najmaden was imprisoned at the U.S. base, the Kurds made a daring attempt to assassinate Dr. Faruk Abdullah Abdurrahman, the newly elected president of the ITF. While returning from meetings in Baghdad, Abdurrahman's entourage was targeted by a massive roadside bomb outside the city of Khalis, about 50 kilometres north of the capital. The main force of the blast hit the car in front of the ITF president. While a number of his bodyguards were seriously wounded, Abdurrahman himself received only slight injuries.

Shortly after returning to Kirkuk, the ITF president was informed of Najmaden's arrest. Accompanying a formal complaint, the ITF issued an ultimatum to the American authorities: either release Najmaden immediately or a violent protest would ensue. While Abdurrahman stopped short of making a direct threat on behalf of his organization, he did suggest that if the Turkmen learned of Najmaden's whereabouts they would take matters into their own hands.

"The people would have stormed the U.S. air base with their bare hands," said Shahin, a 46-year-old schoolteacher I had met in Kirkuk. "All of the Turkmen know about Najmaden's defiance of Saddam for all those years. When he went to prison the first time he said 'you can kill me, but at least I will die a Turkmen.' He is a hero to us."

The ultimatum was enough to convince the Americans to release the political prisoner. On March 18, Najmaden was taken from his cell to the front gate, handed back his clothes, and told to leave the U.S. air base. "They would not even drive me back to my home," he said. "Still, I suppose that a few weeks in an American jail is a more preferable experience than facing a Kurdish execution squad."

Five days after Najmaden's release, Kurdish assassins made an attempt on the life another ITF official in Kirkuk. On March 23, just after 8:00 p.m. and as Dr. Subhi Saber was heading home from work, Kurdish gunmen attacked. Although he escaped injury, his driver, Fazil Kadir, was badly wounded and had to be hospitalized.

I WAS ALSO SADDENED to learn that Dr. Mustafa Kemal had been killed in late May, in a suspicious accident on the highway between Kirkuk and Tuz. I learned of his death when I returned to Kirkuk hoping to interview him. When I arrived at the main ITF headquarters on June 4, I had been surprised to discover that Dr. Abdurrahman and his top officers were all present in Kirkuk. Security was tight as the ITF executive committee was conducting an emergency session.

The U.S. administration had just approved the appointment of Prime Minister Iyad Allawi to take control of the Iraqi Governing Council. Although it was still weeks before the projected July transfer of power, Allawi had revealed the names of his proposed Cabinet. Since September 2003, under the interim authority of U.S. Ambassador Paul Bremer, the Iraqi Governing Council consisted of 25 appointed ministers, only one of whom was a Turkmen. Although Sondul Chapouk was an Iraqi Turkmen, she was not a member of the Iraqi Turkmen Front and represented no party or organization.

During the previous nine months, Dr. Abdurrahman had met repeatedly with both Bremer and, after his appointment, Prime Minister Allawi. Promises had been made that the ITF would have increased representation in the next council, and Allawi told Abdurrahman that he would select three Turkmen as ministers. However, when Allawi read out the 33 names of his new cabinet in May 2004, only two Turkmen had been appointed—Rashad Mandan Omar in the obscure portfolio as the Minister of Technology and Electronics and Bayan Baqer Sulagh as Minister of Reconstruction and Housing. Both Mandan and Sulagh are independent representatives, which left the ITF out of the Iraqi Cabinet altogether.

"When I called Allawi to discuss this betrayal he told me that the matter was not his doing. In the end, Paul Bremer had made the final decisions on the new Cabinet," said

Abdurrahman. "This is not democracy—Bremer is simply the new dictator in Iraq. And now he has made sure that the new council will carry on his wishes after the ceremonial handover."

At an ITF executive meeting, the decision was taken to formally renounce Allawi's new government. "They have already shut us out of the process so we have no choice," explained Dr. Abdurrahman. "We can still work to ensure that we are ready to participate in a truly democratic process, should there be an election in Iraq." Judging from the sombre mood at the meeting, the news of Allawi's cabinet selection had been devastating to the Turkmen. History continued to repeat itself and promises continued to be broken.

It was at this ITF meeting in Kirkuk that I expressed a desire to visit the Turkmen city of Talafar. My request was referred to the organization's executive and, after several minutes of discussion, they asked me where I would stay. As I had never before been to Talafar, I naively said, "Oh, I'll just take a hotel room. Please don't worry about that." The translator looked at me curiously and said, "There are no hotels in Talafar." Somewhat taken aback, I replied, "You mean to tell me that in a city of 400,000 inhabitants there is not a single hotel?" "No," he said, "and there never has been." Dr. Yashar, the head of the ITF in Talafar, cordially invited me to stay at his home. "You will be safe there," he said.

Before arriving in Talafar, I had not really had any concerns for my safety. I knew that all of central Iraq was incredibly volatile, and since the U.S. had ignited the Shiite followers of Muqtada Al-Sadr in April, most of the heretofore dormant south had also become very dangerous for a foreign journalist. But of all the cities in Iraq, I had never heard of any violent

TOP: *Remains of the car bomb that targeted Jalal Azzez (above) at his headquarters in Kirkuk.* **ABOVE LEFT:** *Hal Gurd, the PUK's head of intelligence, believed Turkish intelligence was responsible for the attack.* **LEFT:** *Dr. Faruk Abdurrahman leads the ITF executive. (S. TAYLOR)*

TOP: *Destruction and collateral damage in Sadr City, April 2004. When the U.S. announced its intention to arrest Cleric Muqtada Al-Sadr, the Shiia joined the Sunni Arab Iraqis in open revolt. (SCOTT TAYLOR)* **ABOVE:** *An Abrams tank patrols in the streets of Baghdad. (SCOTT TAYLOR)*

attacks occurring in Talafar. "That is only because the Americans don't report their losses from here, and not a single journalist has bothered to come here," explained Dr. Yashar as we toured the central core of the ancient city.

Pointing to the shattered remains of a large walled compound, Yashar said, "That used to be the American headquarters until it was hit [in July 2003] by a suicide car bomb. Dozens were killed and perhaps 50 wounded. The helicopters were evacuating casualties for hours. But there were never any media reports about it." Following this attack and others, the U.S. authorities eventually abandoned all of their facilities in the city and withdrew their military to the airfield. The former Iraqi air force base is situated approximately five kilometres from the town limits and is completely isolated from the town itself. "Saddam's helicopter gunships could safely operate from there to keep us in line," said Dr. Yashar. "And now the Americans are using the base for the same purpose."

Since July 2003, the resistance in Talafar has increased steadily. "When the U.S. troops first came to Talafar, the Turkmen citizens were very happy to see them because it meant that the terror of Saddam had ended," said Yashar. "But as their vehicles crushed civilian cars, soldiers shot civilians by mistake, and houses were searched at random, we began to resent their presence."

When I visited the Turkmen enclave in June 2004, relations between the people of Talafar and the U.S. military had been severed almost completely. To allow me to walk the streets safely, Yashar had two of his ITF subordinates accompany me at all times. The crowds stared at me with open hostility, and on several occasions my guides had to hurriedly explain that I was a guest of Dr. Yashar's to avoid violence. "I'm sorry but they think you are an American and right away they want to kill you," explained Omar, one of my beleaguered escorts.

When I had requested that a taxi driver take me out to the U.S. airfield, it caused considerable concern among my ITF handlers. We had stopped several cabs to discuss the fare, but all had ended up back at Dr. Yashar's office. "No local driver will take you to the American camp because they don't want to die," said the ITF director. "There are an average of two U.S. soldiers killed in Talafar every week in ambushes and the Americans are eager for revenge. But more dangerous than that is the fact that the resistance fighters watch the air base 24 hours a day. Any Turkmen seen visiting the gate will be presumed to be a traitor and will be killed upon their return home."

That evening, the Yashar family prepared a veritable feast. As is the Turkmen custom, the women cooked the meal and laid out the dining room table for the men to eat first. As we ate, the children brought their friends into the doorway to catch a glimpse of me. Whenever I glanced at them, they would giggle and scatter back to the safety of the kitchen. I realized that in my Western-style suit I must have looked like something from Mars to them. It was a game that would continue well into the night. Once we finished our meal, the men retired to the garden while the women and children ate. As we sat under the stars, many of Talafar's community leaders and intelligentsia came to visit Yashar—and to practice their English on me. The power shortage in Talafar was far more acute than in Baghdad, and in this impoverished city only the wealthiest residents could afford generators. It was a clear night, but without street lights it was eerily dark.

The Turkmen apologised that they could not offer me a

shower after travelling on such a very hot day because Talafar has an acute water shortage. As the population grew over the centuries and Talafar was transformed from a village into a city, the wells and spring-fed streams were unable to meet the increased demand. Plans were drawn to build a pipeline from the Tigris River. Saddam's engineers had actually started construction of the 22-kilometre-long conduit, and sections of pipe had been dropped off all along the Mosul-Kirkuk highway. However, that was just before the 1991 Gulf War and subsequent uprisings.

With sanctions in place, Saddam had neither the material available nor the desire to waste precious resources on the welfare of a potentially disloyal faction and the project was abandoned. To this day, the pipe still sits along the highway. As so water continues to be rationed in Talafar. "It would have taken very little money for the U.S. to have revived the pipeline project and we would have eagerly supplied the workforce," said Yashar. "But we soon learned that the American military was first and foremost concerned with the safety and welfare of its own soldiers—not the Iraqi people."

All of the police and armed security personnel in Talafar are now Turkmen, recruited locally following Saddam's ouster. However, when Iraqi troops discarded their uniforms and fled the Talafar air base in April 2003, the Turkmen had no organized force to replace them. Seeing a power vacuum open up, Kurdish peshmerga from Barzani's KDP quickly pushed into the territory and met no opposition. "They came to loot the Baath regime offices and to steal all the former government vehicles and supplies," said Dr. Yashar. "There were a few small skirmishes when they tried to rob private Turkmen homes, and the Kurds soon knew better than to try and remain inside our city. They took what they could and left."

While the Turkmen of Talafar pride themselves on the fact that the Kurds had made no further attempts to encroach upon their enclave, I would discover that the containment was mutually enforced.

AS MY CAR APPROACHED the checkpoint, my driver became visibly nervous. The soldiers that were searching the cars ahead and questioning the drivers were neither Iraqi police nor American troops, they were KDP peshmerga.

That morning I had hired Mustafa, an ethnic Iraqi Turkmen, to take me to the Turkish border. "Mister, tell them you came today from Mosul or there will be a problem," said Mustafa as we approached the peshmerga. Recognizing my driver as a Turkmen, the Kurdish soldiers were gruff and demanded to know why he was driving a Canadian journalist. My identification papers were taken by an officer and I was ordered out of the car. Several minutes later, I was told to collect my bags and pay Mustafa. He was not allowed to enter this Kurd-controlled area of Iraq, and I was informed that I would be driven 20 kilometres away to the city of Dohuk. There, I would be "processed" by the KDP. Although I protested that I had a flight to catch after crossing the Iraqi-Turkish border and had little time to spare, my arguments were to no avail. "What is the problem?" I asked repeatedly, only to have the peshmerga captain smile broadly each time and reply, "No problem mister."

En route to Dohuk, my Asaish driver-escort, a pot-bellied little man with white hair and bad teeth, questioned me in his broken English: "George Bush is number one, no? Massoud

Barzani good man?" My noncommittal responses prompted him to launch into a diatribe about the regional problems in northern Iraq. "Saddam was bad, but the problem was not only him. Arabs are bad, and Turkmen are bad." As he spat out these words he looked me in the eye to ensure that I was concentrating on his message.

I was already well aware of the post-war inter-ethnic problems in Iraq, but it was my experience that when speaking to the media Kurdish officials would dutifully recite the party line that they were eager to work within a united Iraqi federation. This Asaish agent had no such reservations and instead spoke his mind. Sweeping his arms about to encompass the surrounding landscape, he told me, "This is Kurdistan." And therein revealed the ultimate objective of many Iraqi-Kurds: an independent state.

Arriving at the well protected Asaish headquarters, I was impressed with the scale of the KDP's secret service operation. Funded for the past thirteen years by the CIA, the Asaish had been a valuable American ally in gathering intelligence on Saddam's regime. Now, the very existence of the Asaish and peshmerga were proving somewhat problematic. As Iraqis struggle to build a unified country, there are obviously no clear rules as to the jurisdictional limits of these private armies and intelligence services.

"Under what authority have you detained me?" I asked a senior Asaish officer when I was presented to him. "You are not being detained, you are simply our guest," he explained with a smile. "We want to record the details from your identification."

While I wanted to argue that the seizure of my travel documents at gunpoint could easily be construed as "detention," I settled for asking him what purpose was served by collecting such data from me. "Will this be passed on to the coalition forces or the Iraqi police?" I asked. "You don't understand," replied the officer. "This is our governate, and we are responsible for ensuring that no terrorists enter our territory to bring harm to our people."

After more than an hour, I realized that I was in serious risk of missing my flight. I decided to try and bluff my way out. Demanding to see the Asaish commander, I threatened to inform the Canadian embassy in Ankara that I was being held captive by the KDP in Dohuk. Although I did not have a satellite phone, they had not taken the precaution of searching my bags to be sure. The threat worked like a charm and my passport was hastily returned to me. As a gesture of goodwill, a Kurdish taxi driver was found to replace the long-since departed Mustafa to take me to the border.

In the end, I was able to (just) make my flight, but the experience clearly illustrated that there were still numerous obstacles on the road to rebuilding Iraq. Although continued American tolerance of the peshmerga in northern Iraq may give the false impression of a secure environment, the situation will eventually have to be rectified. Undoubtedly, a violent backlash against the U.S. forces will erupt if they try to forcibly disarm these private Kurdish armies.

But if U.S. President George W. Bush is serious when he talks about bringing "freedom to the people of Iraq," then how can he possibly allow warlords to reign supreme in northern Iraq?

~~~~~~~~~~

POSTSCRIPT

SINCE THE JUNE 28, 2004 handover ceremony in Baghdad, the U.S. continues to stand by its claim that it is committed to bringing democracy to Iraq. The Interim Council headed by Prime Minister Iyad Allawi is only a stepping stone towards an actual election. However, it is difficult to envision how such a polarized constituency—with no prior experience in Western-style democracy—can achieve lasting results with such a short transition period. Furthermore, those individuals able to organize and fund a political campaign already hold leadership positions (either tribal or religious) within the existing framework.

One possibility, given their sheer number, is that the Shiite majority would elect a fundamentalist regime through the democratic process. This scenario seemed so likely that Paul Bremer's administration asked the UN to intervene and postpone the planned elections. It was thought that prominent Shiite Muslim Cleric Al-Sistani would urge his followers to boycott the Western-style elections. This would have eliminated the fundamentalist vote from the equation and allowed a minority coalition of Sunni Arabs and Kurds to form an elected government. Al-Sistani, however, proved to be far cleverer than the Bush administration planners. Realizing that he would win an election if his supporters turned out to vote, Al-Sistani demanded the peoples' right to democracy without further delay and threw Paul Bremer's team into a quandary. The U.S. did not invade Iraq and depose Saddam Hussein in order to allow yet another Iranian-style fundamentalist regime to rise to power in the Middle East. Besides, if such an outcome was to come into being it is more than likely that both the Sunni

Arabs and Kurds would move to secede from Iraq rather than reverse the secular reforms instituted by Saddam's Baath party. What remains to be seen is what sort of democracy the U.S. will eventually try to implement.

In the meantime, Allawi's council is trying to forge a binding constitution which will hamstring any future attempts to impose Islamic fundamentalism on Iraq. Whether the governmental system Iraq adopts is based on individual ridings electing a representative (like in Canada) or on a European system of vote sharing at the federal level where actual party candidates are elected based on their percentage of the vote, the Turkmen of Iraq will benefit by voting as a bloc. This would allow them to elect between eight and ten per cent of the Iraqi parliament, and possibly hold the balance of power between a splinter group made up of the other factions.

While it is difficult to apply Canada's constitutional model to Iraq, the two countries do share certain similarities. While often described as a bilingual nation founded by the English and French, Canada's third founding peoples, are, of course, the First Nations aboriginals. While official bilingualism at a federal level in Iraq would not be practical, there are certainly a number of measures that could be adopted to ensure that the Turkmen (and other Iraqi minorities) have their rights protected by a constitutional authority.

As with the Canadian parliament, regardless of which political party happens to form the government there is always a cabinet minister and government department dedicated to Indian and Northern Affairs. A similar system could be entrenched in the new Iraq, to protect the language, culture and heritage of some 2,000,000 indigenous people. It will take time and international commitment to erase thirty years of Arabification, but this is the only way the Turkmen and the others can maintain their identities.

Ethnic diversity is not something which needs to be eradicated and eliminated. In rebuilding Iraq, the United States owes it to the Iraqi people to tread very carefully so as not to fan the flames of old hatreds or to rekindle religious movements.

Rather than dangling control of Kirkuk in front of the Kurds like a carrot of economic opportunity, the international community would be wise to recognize its long-standing Turkmen origins and composition. To leave any margin of doubt in this regard will only encourage the same sort of ethnic cleansing that has consumed the Balkans over the past decade. By confirming Kirkuk's Turkmen status, the Kurds' impetus for declaring an independent state becomes marginalized and the various factions that reside in northern Iraq would be compelled to work together within some sort of Baghdad-based federal framework.

The Turkmen of Iraq do not want a separate state and are willing to work within a federation—provided they receive the recognition they feel is their long-overdue right. Unfortunately, their hopes for a brighter future remain in doubt as long as they remain listed among "the others."

LEFT: Author Scott Taylor (second from right) poses with Laci Zoldi (second from left) and Asif Sertturkmen (centre) at the September 2003 ITF conference, at which time Dr. Abdurrahman was elected President.

SADDAM HUSSEIN

President of Iraq 1979-2003. When Saddam and the Baath Party toppled President Kassem in 1963, the Turkmen people of Iraq welcomed the new regime with massive demonstrations. However they would soon learn that there was no place for Turkmen representation in the Baathist Governing Council. Although it took a further five years for the Baathists to fully secure their power in Iraq, by the time Saddam pronounced himself President in 1979, his policy of "Arabification" was already full swing. Minorities such as the Turkmen and Kurds were marginalized and their cultural rights were denied. Although many Turkmen fought as conscripts in Saddam's army during the 1980-88 Iran-Iraq War, these same veteran's eagerly took up arms to attempt to oust the Baath Party following the Iraqi army's defeat in Kuwait in 1991.

GEORGE W. BUSH

President of the United States 2001-present. Immediately after he became President in January 2001, Bush made it clear that he intended to oust Saddam Hussein from power in Iraq during his first term in office. After 9/11, the military gears were put in motion which would culminate in the March 2003 invasion of Iraq. It is now apparent that the Bush administration failed to properly plan for the aftermath of removing Saddam's regime. In the lead up to war, Bush was desperate for support-both international allies and internal Iraqi co-operation. To achieve this 'coalition of the willing', the U.S. made a large number of promises which it could not keep in the postwar chaos. The assurances given to the Kurdish warlords in exchange for their assistance has yet to materialize in the form of an independent state with control of Kirkuk's oil riches.

PAUL BREMER

Administrator of the Coalition Provisional Authority (CPA). By May 11, 2003, only 10 days after U.S. President Bush had declared his "mission accomplished" in Iraq, it was already apparent that the post-war plans were falling apart. The original American interim governor- Jay Garner-was relieved of his duties and replaced by the ambitious Paul Bremer, a career diplomat. Bremer soon proved to be in hopelessly over his head. When he handed over power to Prime Minister Iyad Allawi's Governing Council on June 28, 2004, the ceremony was conducted inside the American protected Green Zone. Despite Bremer's constant claims of success, the security situation had worsened to such an extent that the handover was bumped up by 72 hours in order to avoid terrorist attacks. One of the final acts carried out by Bremer was to approve the new Iraqi Council.

MASSOUD BARZANI

Leader of the Kurdistan Democratic Party (KDP). Although technically he is an elected official in northern Iraq's autonomous Kurdistan parliament, in reality Barzani is more akin to a tribal warlord. His father, Chieftain Mulla Barzani, was instrumental in fostering Turkmen-Kurd animosity in the city of Kirkuk in 1959. Since the 1991 Gulf War, the KDP's peshmerga fighters have controlled the provinces of Dohuk and Erbil. In 1996, when the U.S. supported his rival, Jalal Talabani, Barzani cut a separate deal with Saddam Hussein. Iraqi tanks assisted Barzani's troops in pushing into Talabani's area of operation and, in the process, Saddam's operatives were able to successfully dismantle the extensive CIA operation that had been established in northern Iraq. Massoud Barzani was selected by Paul Bremer as a member of the new Iraqi Governing Council.

JALAL TALABANI

President of the Patriotic Union of Kurdistan (PUK). Considered to be more of a hard-line nationalist than his rival Massoud Barzani, the PUK leader has made a number of strange alliances over the past decades. Alternately supported by Iran and the CIA, Talabani also retained loose contacts with the Kurdish funtamentalist group Ansar al-Islam, an organization often connected with the al-Qaeda movement. In order to increase his prominence in the post-war Iraq administration, Talabani had his people stage elaborate 'liberation parades' for the benefit of the Western media and interim U.S. military governor Jay Garner. However, most journalists neglected to mention that the Kurds had already liberated themselves in the 1991 revolt. Talabani's loyalty to the U.S. has resulted in a prominent post in Iraqi Prime Minister Iyad Allawi's interim Cabinet.

DR. SANAN AHMET AGA

Former leader of the Iraqi Turkmen Front (ITF). Although the ITF established its own headquarters in the Kurd-controlled city of Erbil following the post-Gulf War uprising in 1991 in northern Iraq, Aga's organization was never in good standing with Massoud Barzani's local KDP. On the eve of war, Aga attended the U.S. summit in Ankara as the ITF representative. He left those meetings convinced that there would be post-war ethnic violence in Iraq. Following Saddam's ouster in April 2003, Sanan Aga's pre-war compromises with the Baghdad authorities became evident within the ranks of the ITF. Actions taken and decisions made to protect individuals from Saddam's reprisals were now considered to be a political liability by members of the ITF. In September 2003, Aga willingly agreed to step down as President of the ITF to make room for his successor.

DR. FARUK ABDURRAHMAN

President of the Iraqi Turkmen Front (as of September 2003). At the first post war ITF conference held in Kirkuk, Dr. Abdurrahman won a majority mandate from the Turkmen constituency to assume the Presidency. Immediately following his election, Faruk began lobbying for increased Turkmen representation on the new Iraqi Governing Council. Although the ITF President appealed to the international community and met with prominent Iraqi political leaders, he was unable to secure any support from U.S. Ambassador Paul Bremer. Although newly appointed Prime Minister Iyad Allawi had promised Faruk he would appoint no less than three ITF members to his Cabinet, in the end the ITF was completely shut out of the Iraqi political process. Faruk now hopes to establish a Turkmen voice through the promised "democratic" election of January 2005.

IYAD ALLAWI

Prime Minister of Iraq (as of June 28, 2004-present). Appointed by U.S. Governor Paul Bremer, to head to interim Iraqi Council, Allawi has so far proven to be little more than an American puppet. Immediately following the ouster of Saddam Hussein, the U.S. installed Ambassador Paul Bremer to run Iraq with the assistance of 25 hand-picked appointees, who formed the Iraqi Governing Council. This group had no independent powers and answered directly to Bremer as Administrator of the Coalition Provisional Authority (CPA). Following the handover of power to Iyad Allawi's new council, Iraqis now have more autonomy, however, security issues remain under the control of the Pentagon. In August 2004, Allawi named a further 80 parliamentarians to his government. Although eight Turkmen were chosen, Dr. Abdurrahman is the only ITF representative.

ZALMAY KHALILZAD

U.S. Special Envoy to Northern Iraq. Just prior to the 2003 military intervention, President Bush appointed Khalilzad as his special representative to broker a binding deal with the various ethnic/political factions in northern Iraq. The Afghan-born Khalilzad was a close confidante of Deputy Secretary of Defense Paul Wolfowitz, who is regarded as one of the Bush administration's most hawkish advisors. In March 2003, in an effort to broker a post-war settlement, Khalilzad held an eleventh-hour summit in Ankara, Turkey, for all of the major northern Iraqi stakeholders. All of those present knew that the promises made by Khalilzad on behalf of the States would never be upheld and the consensus was one of distrust for U.S. policy. "[Khalilzad] has promised the same carrot to all of the assembled donkeys," said one delegate.

DONALD RUMSFELD

United States Secretary of Defense. "Rummy's" first experience in Iraq was in the mid-80s when he was Ronald Reagan's special envoy to Iraq, which, at that time, was a useful ally in undermining the Iranian fundamentalist movement. When Saddam wanted to pull out of the Iran-Iraq War due to escalating casualties, Rumsfeld had promised to deliver to Iraq whatever support was necessary to continue fighting —including the sale of chemical weapons. But prior to the intervention in 2003, Rumsfeld demonized Saddam as "evil" for having used chemical weapons to quell the Kurd uprising while neglecting to mention the U.S. had sold them to Iraq in the late 1980s. Although the post-war sex abuse scandal at Abu Ghraib rocked the Pentagon, President Bush maintained that Rumsfeld was doing a "superb job" in Iraq.

PAUL WOLFOWITZ

United States Deputy Secretary of Defense. Undeniably the leading 'hawk' on Bush's war team, Wolfowitz had first advocated Saddam's removal during the 1991 Gulf War. A protégé of then-CIA Director George Bush Sr., Wolfowitz accelerated his career by heading up Special Project B, which revised intelligence data (in the final days of the Cold War) to portray the Soviet Union as far more of a military threat than it was. President Reagan used these revised documents to justify increased defense spending until the USSR collapsed. It was later revealed that Wolfowitz's dossier had been "sexed up" in a fashion similar to the reports used to justify the attack on Iraq in 2003. Wolfowitz was under the mistaken belief that Iraq is just one people. He was also wrong when he said U.S. troops would be greeted as liberators.

DICK CHENEY

Vice President of the United States. Like Rumsfeld and Wolfowitz, Cheney had a long history in dealing with Saddam Hussein since he was Secretary of Defense during the first Gulf War. While the Republicans were out of power during the Clinton era, Cheney solidified his extensive corporate contracts within the U.S. military industrial complex. Even before the first bomb fell on Iraq on March 20, 2003, Cheney's former employer, Kellog, Brown and Root, had been issued substantial contracts to support the U.S. forces deployed to the Persian Gulf and in the reconstruction of Iraq. One of Kellog, Brown and Root's major accounts was the Iraqi exile training facility in Taszar, Hungary. Unfortunately, the exile training program proved a costly failure, turning out only 80 recruits before being cancelled by the CIA.

ANCIENT MESOPOTAMIA

Considered to be the "Cradle of Civilization," the lands between the Tigris and Euphrates Rivers were the birthplace of many powerful empires and subject to numerous invasions. The history of the Iraqi Turkmen is inexorably interwoven throughout these social, political and military developments.

SUMER (3500BC – 2400BC)

The ancient empire of Sumer was located in the region of southern Mesopotamia. Although there are no exact dates recorded, it is believed that the first Turkmen presence settled in Mesopotamia around 3500BC. Sumer was a linguistic and ethnic mosaic that included earlier inhabitants of the region. Initially, the Turkmen involved in this first phase of migration resisted assimilation. However, over the passage of time, the relatively small Turkic tribes became absorbed by the more numerous indigenous population. Considered to be the "Cradle of Civilization," the Sumerians were the first people known to have devised a scheme of written representation

as a means of communication. The most important political development of this era was the emergence of kings, who exercised absolute political authority over the Sumerian city-states.

AKKAD (2400BC – 2200BC)

Sumer was conquered in 2334BC by Sargon I, king of the Semitic city of Akkad. To ensure his supremacy, Sargon created the first conscripted army, a development necessitated by the need to mobilize large numbers of labourers for irrigation and flood-control works. The fall of the Akkadians was caused by the re-emergence of the Sumerians, under the King of Ur, who briefly established hegemony over much of Mesopotamia. However, by 2000BC, combined attacks by the Amorites, a Semitic people from the west, and the Elamites, a Caucasian people from the east, had destroyed the Third Dynasty of Ur. The invaders, nevertheless, retained much of the Sumerian-Akkadian political and cultural legacy.

BABYLON (2000BC – 539BC)

The Amorites, a prosperous nomadic tribe, emerged as the dominant political power sometime before 2000BC and established cities on the Tigris and the Euphrates rivers. They chose Babylon, a town to the north, as their capital. However, widespread migration of tribes from central Asia would soon destabilize the Babylonian empire. Around 1600BC, Indo-European-speaking tribes invaded India; while other tribes settled in Iran and eastern Europe. One of these groups, the Hittites, allied itself with the Kassites, a warlike, nomadic people of unknown origins. Together, they conquered and destroyed Babylon. After 800BC, the Semitic-speaking Assyrians from northern Mesopotamia embarked on a policy of expansion. In 612BC, revolts of subject peoples combined with the allied forces of two new kingdoms, those of the Medes and the Chaldeans (Neo-Babylonians), to effectively end Assyrian rule. This new regime would last just half a century before falling to yet another invader, the Persian King Cyrus the Great who captured Babylon and added Mesopotamia to his empire in the year 539 B.C.

PERSIAN AND GREEK INTRUSIONS (551BC – 331BC)

Persian Iranian rule lasted for more than 200 years, from 551BC to 331BC. During this time, large numbers of Persian tribes were added to Mesopotamia's ethnically diverse population. Persian rule ended at the hands of Alexander the Great who led a Greek army into Iraq. After his death in 311BC his empire was divided. Iraq was the share of Seleicus who established the Seleviad dynasty with his capital at Babylon. In the centuries to come, the Pathian, Persians, and Sasanians would occupy the Cradle of Civilization. Eventually the city of Babylon would lose its preeminence as the center of the civilized world as political and economic activity shifted to the Mediterranean and Rome.

ARAB CONQUEST AND THE COMING OF ISLAM

Islamic forays into Iraq began during the reign of Caliph Abu Bakr. In 634AD, an army of 18,000 Arab tribesmen, reached the delta of the Tigris and Euphrates. Although the occupying Persian force was vastly superior in tactics and numbers, its soldiers were exhausted from their unremitting campaigns against the Byzantines. Many of the Iraqi tribes were Christian at the time

of the Islamic conquest. By 650AD, Muslim armies under the command of Ubaydullah Bin Ziyad had reached the Amu Darya (Oxus River) and had conquered all of Mesopotamia. One of the keys to Bin Ziyad's success was the use of Turkmen archers from Central Asia. Following the conquest of Mesopotamia, approximately 2000 Turkmen soldiers were deployed around Basra.

THE ABBASID CALIPHATE (750-1055)

During the reign of the first seven Caliphs, Baghdad became the centre of power where Arab and Persian cultures merged. This era is remembered throughout the Arab world and by Iraqis in particular, as the pinnacle of the Islamic past. Turkish recruitment into the army strengthened the Abbasid Caliphate. Caliph Al Mansour (754-775) established a regiment consisting entirely of Turkmen. These troops continued to have a growing influence in the Abbasid army. More than 70,000 Turkmen troops with their families settled in Baghdad under the Caliphs.

THE SELJUK-PERIOD (1055-1258)

The Seljuks are originally from the Oguz Turkic tribes of Central Asia. These Turkmen had established a great empire from India to Egypt and from the west coast of Turkey to Oman. The Seljuk Empire was extended to Syria and Palestine in 1089, During this period many Turkmen dynasties were established and Turkmen families were settled in the Tavuk region, south of Kirkuk. Ruling from their capital in Baghdad, the Seljuk's controlled the lands from the Bosphorus to Chinese Turkestan until approximately 1155. The Seljuks continued to expand their territories, but they were content to let the local tribesmen sim-

Sultan Selim I expanded the Ottoman empire to the east. In 1515, he destroyed the Persian Army, opening the way for his successors to conquer Mesopotamia.

foundation of the Abbasid culture to the tribes of the river valleys.

THE OTTOMAN PERIOD
(1534-1914)

In the years following the Mongol invasion, Turkmen tribes from Iran, the Safavids, struggled for control of Iraq with the advancing Ottomans under Suleiman the Magnificent. Baghdad fell to Suleiman in 1534. The Ottomans divided Iraq into four provinces which they would govern until the First World War. One major impact of the Safavid-Ottoman conflict on Iraqi history was the deepening of the Shia-Sunni religious divisions. Another important development during this period was the aggressive expansion of European colonial and economic interests in the Middle East. The British had established a consulate at Baghdad in 1802, and a French consulate followed shortly thereafter. European interest in modernizing Iraq to facilitate Western commercial interests coincided with Ottoman reforms. In 1908, a new ruling clique, the Young Turks, took power in Istanbul. They stressed secular politics and patriotism over the pan-Islamic ideology preached by Sultan Abd al Hamid. However, the Turkish Empire was in a slow decline. By the early 20th century, the once powerful Ottoman Empire was referred to as the "Sick Old Man of Europe."

– compiled by Donna Tillotson

ply pay tribute while administering and ruling their own lands. Tughril (1177-94), the last Seljuk sultan of Iraq, was killed by the leader of another Turkic dynasty, the Khwarizm Shah. Before he could establish his rule, however, Iraq was overrun by the Mongol horde.

THE MONGOL INVASION

In the early years of the thirteenth century, a powerful Mongol leader named Temujin brought together an alliance of the Mongol tribes and led them on a devastating sweep through China, eastern Europe and the Middle East. In Mesopotamia, political chaos, severe economic depression, and social disintegration followed in the wake of the Mongol invasions. Baghdad, once the centre of a great empire, rapidly lost its importance. Basra, which had been a key transit point for global sea trade, was circumvented after the Portuguese found an alternative maritime route to Asia around Cape of Good Hope. By the end of the Mongol period, the focus of Mesopotamian society had shifted from the urban

MODERN IRAQ

1914 – In order to protect its oil interests in neighbouring Iran, the British launch an offensive into Mesopotamia against the Ottoman Turks.

1915 – After some initial success against the Turks near Basra, the British expeditionary forces push north where they suffer a devastating defeat at the city of Kut.

1917 – With additional reinforcements and the assistance of Arab allies, the Turks are pushed out of Mesopotamia and the British occupy the provinces of Basra and Baghdad.

1918 – Although it was not previously known that the Turk-occupied Mesopotamian provinces possessed oil resources, by the end of World War I British naval engineers had determined that this region contained "the worlds largest deposits." At the end of hostilities, the Turkish army still controlled the province of Mosul, including Kirkuk. However, in the post war collapse of the Ottoman Empire. The British violated the armistice and occupied the rest of Mesopotamia.

1919 – With proven oil reserves located in Basra, the British hesitate on turning this region over to the Arabs as they had previously promised.

1920 – After being snubbed by both Britain and France, Faisal I declares himself the King of Syria and his brother Abdullah is named the King of Mesopotamia. The French and British suppress Faisal and ignore Abdullah, setting in motion a regional wave of violence and anarchy.

1921 – Unable to suppress the revolt in Mesopotamia, the exiled King Faisal I is recalled from Lebanon and proclaimed 'King' of the newly created State of Iraq.

The collapse of the Ottoman Empire coincided with the discovery of oil in Iraq, thus setting the stage for a century of violent unrest and conflict.

1924 - A British 'show of force' in Kirkuk results in Arab 'levies' massacring Turkmen citizens.

1927 – The natural gas fires of Baba Gur Gur are finally explored and the oil deposits of northern Iraq are proven to be among the world's richest.

1932 – King Faisal I attains Iraq's independence from Britain. Iraq is admitted into the League of Nations, but British troops and aircraft remain in the country which has now been declared a protectorate.

1938 – Oil is discovered in the sheikdom of Kuwait and Faisal's son, King Ghazi, lays claim to this territory as Iraq's 19th province. With both Kuwait and Iraq under British protection, the issue of Kuwait's appropriation is soon dropped.

1939 – King Ghazi is killed in a suspicious automobile accident. His three-year-old son, Faisal II, assumes the throne with his uncle, Abdul Illah, serving as regent.

1941 – At the height of World War II, with British troops stretched thin around the globe, Iraqi military officers stage a rebellion. The British rush reinforcements from India and Palestine to restore Faisal II's

Saddam Hussein became President of Iraq in 1979.

monarchy and secure British oil investments.

1958 – General Abdul Karim Kassem stages a military coup. King Faisal II is killed and the last of the British troops are withdrawn from Iraq.

1959 – On the anniversary of President Kassem's coup, the Kurds stage an ambush against Turkmen demonstrators in Kirkuk. 25 Turkmen political activist are killed and dozens wounded.

1963 – With the backing of the CIA, the Baath party seize power briefly. In the wake of the coup, President Kassem and thousands of his followers are slaughtered.

1968 – Although they had in turn been ousted from power by a military junta, the Baathists regain control of Iraq. As deputy to President Ahmed Hasa Al-Bakr, young Saddam Hussein was seen as the controlling force in Iraq.

1972 – Iraq nationalizes its oil resources and calls on other Arab nations to do the same.

1973 – The Organization of Petroleum Exporting Countries (OPEC) raises prices to protest America's support of Israel in the Yom Kippur War. This sets the U.S. economy into turmoil.

1975 – After the CIA and the Shah of Iran had successfully supported a Kurdish rebellion in Iraq, Saddam signed a treaty in Algeria. In exchange for Iran's use of the Shatt al-Arab waterway, Iraq's military was allowed a free hand to crush the Kurds.

1979 – Saddam Hussein becomes President of Iraq at the same time the Shah of Iran is toppled. With Shiite fundamentalists in control of Iran, Saddam is encouraged by the U.S. State Department to declare war against the Ayatollah Khomeini.

1980 – Saddam believes his forces can easily defeat the Iranian army since it had been recently purged of its officers corps. However, after only limited initial gains, the Iraqi offensive bogs down into a war of attrition.

1984 – With his forces pushed back against the Shatt al-Arab, Saddam indicates he will end the war. President Ronald Reagan's special envoy, Donald Rumsfeld, flies to Baghdad. Saddam is promised full U.S. support – including chemical weaponry.

1988 – Iran and Iraq sign a peace agreement. The Pentagon begins conducting war games based on the scenario that Iraq has attacked Kuwait.

1990 – Forced to repay Kuwait a $30 billion loan yet unable to increase oil prices, Iraq issues an ultimatum to Kuwait to cease its overproduction of oil. The U.S. advises Saddam that it has no position on Arab-Arab affairs. On August 2, Iraq invades Kuwait. Four days later the UN Security Council imposes sanctions against

On January 17, 1991 the U.S. coalition air force began a 48-day air campaign of systematic destruction against Iraq.

***

1998 – The U.S. passes the Iraq Liberation Act in October. In December, UN weapons inspectors are withdrawn from Baghdad. This precipitates assassination attempts against Saddam in the form of "leadership target" airstrikes.

Iraq. On August 7, George Bush Sr. launches *Operation Desert Shield*.

1991 – On January 17, the U.S.-led coalition initiates 48 days of airstrikes against Iraq and occupied Kuwait. On February 24, the ground assault goes in and Saddam's forces are routed. Four days later, Iraq signs a ceasefire agreement with the coalition forces. With the collapse of his army, Saddam faces rebellion within Iraq. After months of heavy fighting, Saddam regains 15 of his 18 provinces; the three northern provinces remain under the control of Kurdish rebels. Many Turkmen who had supported the rebellion are forced to flee their homes.

1996 – Saddam assists Kurdish warlord Massoud Barzani in an incursion into the territory controlled by rival Kurd, Jalal Talabani. In the process, Saddam destroys a CIA operation in northern Iraq. After 6 years of sanctions, the Iraqi people have suffered nearly 1.5 million deaths. As a result, the United Nations eases the embargo and initiates the oil-for-food program. Saddam's exports are completely controlled by the UN, which allows him to buy only food and medicine.

2000 – Saddam meets with Venezuelan President Hugo Chavez to discuss the strategy of trading their oil exports in the new Euro currency rather than the U.S. dollar.

2001 – On February 17, newly elected President George W. Bush sends a message to Saddam in the form of airstrikes. The world condemns the U.S. aggression. On September 11, the U.S. suffers a devastating terror attack. Saddam issues a statement proclaiming that America has "reaped what it has sown." Although Osama bin Laden is the primary suspect, Bush warns Saddam to "watch his step."

2002 – On August 15, the U.S. Joint Chiefs of Staff approve a strategic plan to invade Iraq. On October 15, Saddam stages a presidential referendum and wins a 100 per cent majority. On November 20, Iraq agrees to readmit inspectors and turns over its weapons dossier to the UN on December 6. UN chief weapons inspector Hans Blix labels the dossier "incomplete."

2003 – On January 27, Hans Blix tables his final report. The following day President Bush denounces Iraq's "lack of cooperation" in his State of the Union address. After they fail to win consensus among the UN Security Council members, the U.S., Britain and Spain announce on March 10 that they will proceed against Iraq without a second UN resolution. On March 18, President Bush delivers an ultimatum to Saddam: Leave Iraq within 48 hours or face the consequences.

THE WAR IN IRAQ

On April 9, 2003, all Iraqi resistance suddenly collapsed.

MARCH 20, 2003 – Baghdad is blasted by a massive aerial bombardment described by the Pentagon as a "leadership strike."

MARCH 23, 2003 – Coalition forces meet little initial resistance, but Iraqi defenses stiffen around the city of Nasiriya. The U.S. 507th Maintenance Company is ambushed leaving 10 killed, 50 wounded and 12 taken prisoner.

APRIL 6, 2003 – U.S. forces seize Baghdad's Saddam International airport. On the northern front, the allied Kurdish militia launches an offensive towards Kirkuk. U.S. jets mistake the Kurdish advance for Iraqis and 18 Kurds are killed in a friendly fire incident.

APRIL 8, 2003 – All Iraqi army resistance collapses unexpectedly. Kurdish troops enter Mosul and Kirkuk. The Peshmerga are intent on burning all government records such as birth certificates and land registry titles.

APRIL 9, 2003 – Although irregular Arab Fedayeen fighters retain control of most of Baghdad, the U.S. Marines assist a group of Iraqi exiles in pulling down a statue of Saddam in Firdos Square. CNN proclaims Saddam's regime "toppled."

APRIL 10, 2003 – In the absence of law and order, widespread looting and arson erupts throughout Iraq. While critics chastise the Americans forces for not quelling the riots, U.S. Secretary of Defense Donald Rumsfeld says that Iraqis are simply "enjoying their freedom."

During the short military campaign and anarchy that followed the collapse of Saddam's regime, Iraqi civilians paid a heavy price.

George Bush called an end to combat operations on May 1, 2003, but the Iraqi resistance continued to fight.

The U.S. captures Iraq's former vice-president, Taha Yassin Ramadan, but the attacks continue. The UN, Red Cross and other aid agencies begin pulling their personnel out of an "unsafe" Iraq.

MAY 1, 2003 – Aboard USS *Abraham Lincoln*, George W. Bush announces a victory in Iraq and that "all major combat operations" have ceased. Looting and sporadic resistance continue unabated. U.S. commanders say the rampant violence is *not* organized and *not* a guerrilla war.

MAY 2, 20036 – It is announced that interim U.S. military governor Jay Garner will be replaced by former diplomat Paul Bremer. Although the State Department denies Garner was fired, it is a sign that America's original postwar plan is rapidly falling apart.

JULY 2, 2003 – After Iraqis launch a series of deadly ambushes, President Bush challenges the rebels to "bring it on." U.S. commanders now admit they are engaged in a guerilla war – but deny that Iraq is a potential quagmire.

JULY 23, 2003 – With attacks against U.S. forces still escalating, the Americans succeed in killing Saddam's two sons – Uday and Qusay – after a shootout in Mosul. American commanders now use the word *quagmire* to define the worsening situation – but deny that Iraq will become another Vietnam.

AUGUST 19, 2003 – A massive car bomb explodes at the UN compound in Baghdad, killing 20 and injuring 40 aid workers.

AUGUST 28, 2003 – The death of a U.S. soldier brings the post-war American death toll to 139 – one more than during actual combat operations. Not included in this total are non-U.S. coalition forces and American-funded Iraqi security guards who have also lost their lives in Iraq.

NOVEMBER, 2003- Major fighting erupts in Fallujah, and the resistance forces the 82nd Airborne to withdraw from the city limits.

FEBRUARY 1, 2004- Twin suicide attacks in Erbil target the headquarters of Massoud Barzani and rival Jalal Talabani. Casualties exceed 65 killed and 200 wounded.

APRIL 4, 2004- U.S. forces announce their intention to capture radical Shiite cleric Muqtada Al-Sadr, and simultaneously launch a counter offensive against the Sunni stronghold of Fallujah. All of Iraq erupts in violence as Al-Sadr's militia take control of several religious sites.

JUNE 3, 2004- Newly appointed Prime Minister Iyad Allawi announces his new cabinet. Only one Turkmen is named to the 30 member council and is not a representative from the ITF.

JUNE 28, 2004- Three days ahead of schedule, the U.S. authorities hand over power to Allawi's interim Iraqi council.

Index

Other books published by Esprit de Corps Books

SPINNING ON THE AXIS OF EVIL: America's War Against Iraq
By Scott Taylor

Spinning on the Axis of Evil is based on Scott Taylor's personal experiences and observations gathered during 14 separate trips into Iraq – before and after the toppling of Saddam's regime. This book provides a rare insight into the plight of the Iraqi people who suffered through three devastating wars and 13 years of crippling sanctions. From clandestine talks with Saddam's top intelligence officials to dinner table chats with ordinary citizens, Taylor reveals what it was like to be inside Iraq during the dramatic countdown to Bush's declaration of war. *Spinning on the Axis of Evil* is a scathing indictment of those who used falsehoods to justify a war – and failed to plan for its horrific aftermath.
ISBN: 1-895896-22-3 / *Retail Price:* $21.99
Details: 232 pages (including 16 colour pages), trade paperback, photos, index, chronology, biographies of political figures

DIARY OF AN UNCIVIL WAR: The Violent Aftermath of the Kosovo Conflict
By Scott Taylor

The June 1999 entry of NATO troops was hailed as the "Liberation of Kosovo" by the western media – most of whom promptly packed up and headed home from the Balkans. This declaration of victory was naive and premature given the Alliance's objectives of deposing Yugoslav President Slobodan Milosevic and creating a safe, multi-ethnic environment in Kosovo. Rather than ending the civil strife, NATO's intervention set in motion a series of events that would have violent repercussions throughout Serbia, Kosovo and Macedonia. This book – consisting primarily of the author's first-hand observations and interviews with the people and players involved in this crisis – is a very personal account of war and its aftermath in Serbia and Macedonia.
ISBN: 1-895896-20-7 / *Retail Price:* $19.99
Details: 208 pp, paperback, photos, index, chronology, biographies of key political figures

INAT: Images of Serbia and the Kosovo Conflict
By Scott Taylor

For 25 days in May and June 1999, Scott Taylor reported on the NATO air campaign from inside Yugoslavia. As one of the few western journalists to be granted such access, Taylor was able to gain a unique perspective to the Kosovo conflict: the Serbian side.
INAT chronicles the NATO air raids; the on-again, off-again peace talks; Russia's sudden race into Kosovo; the NATO (KFOR) deployment; the retreat of the Yugoslavian army; the flight of Serbian refugees; and the bitter aftermath of the war on a bomb-ravaged Serbia.
ISBN: 1-895896-10-X / *Retail Price:* $16.99
Details: 160 pp, trade paperback, photos, index, chronology, biographies of political figures

SHADOW WARS: Special Forces in the New Battle Against Terrorism
By David Pugliese

Special Forces units around the world have played a critical, though often secretive role since war was declared on global terrorism following the September 11 attacks on the United States. Now, through compelling narrative and explosive photos, *Shadow Wars* reveals how these units are leading the fight. From the rugged mountains of Afghanistan to the vast deserts of Iraq, *Shadow Wars* details operations by U.S. Army Green Berets and Delta Force, U.S. Navy SEALs, Air Force and CIA special operations troops, along with Australia's Special Air Service, the British SAS and SBS, Poland's GROM, Canada's JTF2 as well as highly-controversial raid by Russia's Alpha Group to rescue hostages held by Chechen terrorists in Moscow in the fall of 2002. *Shadow Wars* brings together more than 80 photos of special forces in action, some never before made public.

ISBN: 1-895896-24-X / Retail Price: $21.99

Details: *208 pages (including 16 colour pages),* trade paperback, photos, source-notes, glossary, index

CANADA'S SECRET COMMANDOS: The Unauthorized Story of Joint Task Force Two
By David Pugliese

Award-winning journalist David Pugliese tells you everything the government doesn't want you to know about the most secret unit in the Canadian military today – Joint Task Force Two. *Canada's Secret Commandos* goes behind the scenes in uncovering the missions, training and inner workings of this country's version of the SAS. It reveals the unit's most secretive plans, including details about a bid to rescue Canadian peacekeepers held hostage in Bosnia, an even more dangerous scheme to launch an attack on terrorists in Peru and commando missions in Nepal and the Central African Republic. It also details highly-secretive operations at home against militant native groups such as the Mohawk Warrior Society in Ontario and Quebec as well as natives in British Columbia.

ISBN: 1-895896-18-5 / Retail Price: $21.99

Details: *232 pp, trade paperback, photos, source-notes, glossary, index*

For more information on Esprit de Corps and its many products,
visit our web site at www.espritdecorps.ca or contact us directly at our main office.

Esprit de Corps Books
#204 - 1066 Somerset Street West, Ottawa, Ontario, Canada K1Y 4T3
Tel: (613) 725-5060 / Fax: (613) 725-1019
e-mail: espritdecorp@idirect.com
www.espritdecorps.ca

EPILOGUE

In September 2004, following the completion of this manuscript, the author ventured back into northern Iraq to report on the escalating violence in Talafar. The tensions between the resistance and U.S. forces that Scott Taylor had observed during his visit to the Turkmen enclave only two months before, had erupted into a full-scale uprising. The intial media reports were sketchy and contradictory at best. But Taylor felt that his earlier association with Turkmen officials in the embattled city would allow him to make a more accurate assessment of the situation. What he did not know was that the perpetrators of this rebellion were in fact Islamic extremists, a chapter of the Ansar al-Islam. As a result, he found himself taken hostage by the mujahedeen and forced to endure five days of beatings and torture. This is his story.

7:16 P.M., SEPTEMBER 7, 2004, TALAFAR, IRAQ — It was nearly dusk when we arrived at the city outskirts of Talafar. On the main highway to Mosul, about a dozen Iraqi policemen at a checkpoint were supervising a frightened exodus of civilian refugees. For the past week there had been media reports of escalating violence between resistance fighters and U.S. troops in Talafar, and already many of the residents had fled the embattled city. From American services in the Mosul Airfield, I had learned earlier that day that a major U.S. offensive was about to begin. The Americans had reinforced their local garrison with an additional battalion of armour and infantry and I was advised that within days, the U.S. military was going to 'clean house' in Talafar.

It was my intention to enter the city before it was shut down, and then send reports about the civilian casualties and possible humanitarian crisis that would result from a major battle.

Admittedly, it had not been easy to find a taxi driver willing to take me to Talafar. All the drivers in Mosul had been warned that the mujahedeen were in control of the city — and that it was "too dangerous." One Kurdish fellow disagreed with his colleagues and said that their fears were unfounded. With daylight fading, we quickly made a bargain on the fare and set off.

Talafar is an almost entirely Turkmen enclave in northwestern Iraq. I had just finished writing a book about the history of these Turkish-speaking indigenous Iraqis. As part of my research, I had visited Talafar in June and felt that if I could just reach my known contacts, I would be safe among friends. I knew there would be some risk involved — particularly once the Americans attacked — but I planned to observe the fighting from a safe house, well away from any actual combat.

The sight of U.S. paid Iraqi police forces monitoring traffic had seemed like a good sign that things were still under control, despite the recent fighting. As I did not have an exact address for my previous contact, I approached a police checkpoint to ask for assistance. When I asked them to be taken "to Dr. Yashar," they recognized his name as a prominent local Turkmen official and eagerly nodded in the affirmative. A senior policeman was summoned and he instructed me and Zeynep Tugrul, a Turkish journalist who was serving as my translator, and filing her own reports for *Sabah*, a daily national newspaper, to climb into a nearby car containing four masked gunman. As we clambered into the backseat, one of the gunmen said in excellent English, "We will take you to Doctor Yashar. Please do not be afraid."

I had presumed that these men were some sort of special police force — our own Canadian counter-terrorists teams often wear ski-masks — so I had no immediate cause for concern. However, as soon as we entered Talafar, I saw that the streets were full of similarly masked resistance fighters armed with Kalashnikov rifles and RPGs (rocket-propelled grenades). I suddenly realized we were in the hands of the resistance. Still believing that they were taking me to my friend's house, instead we were ushered into a small courtyard outside a walled two-story building. There were about a half dozen armed men inside, none of them smiling.

As soon as the metal door clanged shut behind us, the English–speaking leader said, "You are spies... and now you are prisoners." All of our cameras, equipment and identification were taken from us and we were told to sit on a mat with our backs to the wall. "The Americans will attack soon and I have to see to my men," said our captor. "I will deal with you when I return."

Shortly after nightfall, they brought a platter of food into the compound, and in what would soon become a routine pattern, they served us first be-

fore eating dinner themselves. Admittedly I did not have much of an appetite.

The plates had just been cleared away when another car pulled up outside and four more gunmen came quickly through the door. Before I could
even react, I was pulled to my feet and pressed against the wall with my
hands on top of my head. Almost immediately I heard the distinct sound of
a Kalashnikov being cocked about a metre behind me. In fear and shock at
the realization that they were about to execute me, Zeynep screamed at
them in Turkish: "Don't shoot him… he has a son!"

The outburst was enough to distract them momentarily and they began to explain to her the necessity of killing a "Jewish spy." Thankfully, I
had no idea what was being said. The brief discussion was still taking place
when our original captor returned. Harsh words were exchanged between
the two groups of gunmen, and it seemed as though a prisoner's fate was
the proprietorship of those who made the capture: The would-be execu-
tioners left.

It was at this point that Zeynep was blindfolded and taken away for
questioning. The remaining guards — their ages ranging from 15 to 50 —
took alternating turns between watching me and crouching behind the second–floor parapet and looking in the sky for signs of the imminent U.S.
attack.

About two hours later, it was my turn to be blindfolded and roughly
manhandled into what felt to be an SUV or Land Rover. At the second house,
I was rushed through several doorways and up several stairs. With my
hands tied behind my back and unable to see, I stumbled and fell several
times only to be pulled forcibly back to my feet and once again shoved
forward. "Hurry, hurry, you bastard Jew," whispered one of my guards as
he slammed my head into a doorframe.

I was forced to lie face down on a mat, and two men carefully searched
through all of my pockets. Finding my money inside my sock (about $700
U.S.) they laughed and said, "Your money is our money — you won't need
cash in Heaven."

It was difficult to gauge how long I laid there in the dark, but my shoulders were aching when they finally untied my hands and brought me to
another room for interrogation. My blindfold was removed and they shone
a bright flashlight directly in my eyes. "Which intelligence agency are you

working for?" began the questioning. For about one hour I did my best to answer all their allegations and explain to them my intentions for going to Talafar was as a journalist. Two men were questioning me. In what seemed like a bad Hollywood comedy, someone started up a generator outside and, the lights came back on and the two interrogators clumsily tried to pull their ski-masks back on before I could recognize their faces.

With the tension broken, the one who had identified himself as "Emir" (leader) actually started to laugh and left his mask off. This man had been among the group that had taken us at the police checkpoint. "Sleep now and I will check your story. If you are telling the truth, we will release you — if not, you die," he said.

IT WAS ABOUT 6 A.M. the following morning when I was kicked awake, rolled onto my stomach, blindfolded and bound. This time they transported Zeynep and I at the same time. Although the vehicle had roared through the deserted streets at top speed, you could hear the engines of U.S. unmanned aircraft flying overhead, watching every move made by the resistance. Knowing that these "Predators" have the capability to not only transmit video images but also launch guided missiles, I felt incredibly vulnerable during that short drive. At the third house, our blindfolds were removed and we were fed a generous breakfast of fried eggs and flatbread. After a cup of tea, I was escorted to a small room with barred windows. There were three guards at this facility which appeared to be a small house or workshop. Two were middle-aged men while the other was just a 15-year-old boy. They were obviously not frontline mujahedeen, but were still supportive of the resistance.

In the first hours, they had been very strict in enforcing the rules. I was to sit on a broken chair in the middle of my cell. However, as the temperature rose to about 45° Celsius and my sun-baked room turned into an oven, they had compassionately allowed me to venture outside. By nightfall everyone was so relaxed that Zeynep and I sat eating dinner and talking to our guards. The young boy stated that his only ambition in life was to "die a martyr." Shortly past dark, the Emir returned and informed us that he had confirmed that we were not spies. He gave a 'Muslim promise' to set us free in the morning. On this night Zeynep and I would remain his 'guests'. We were also about to become front-row spectators to an intense battle between the resistance and U.S. forces.

JUST PAST MIDNIGHT, AMERICAN Apache helicopters attacked. Their arrival over Talafar was greeted by a heavy barrage of RPG and cannon fire. We could hear the distinctive 'crack', 'whump' sounds of the Iraqi rocket grenades being launched and then deafening bursts of fire from the Apaches.

From inside the workshop's courtyard, we could not see the battle's progress, but from the sounds of the gunfire we could plot its course. On several occasions, the mujahedeen fighters all across the city would scream out "Allah akbar! Allah akbar!" (God is great!) I had first thought that these cries were in response to them downing a helicopter, but our young guard explained that they were cheering the deaths of their own, newly created martyrs.

At about 3 a.m. there was a loud banging on the courtyard gate. Our guards let a mujahedeen fighter inside, and he spoke quickly with them in Turkish. Hurriedly a storeroom was opened and the fighter helped himself to three RPGs, which he tucked inside his belt. I could see inside the small room, which was literally packed with munitions, and I realized that we were being held captive in one of the resistance's ammo depots. The fighter took a bowl of water, drank thirstily, then rushed back out onto the darkened streets. Minutes later he began firing from a rooftop about fifty metres away. He had only managed to launch two of his rockets before he disappeared in a burst of 25 mm cannon fire from an Apache which literally blew him into pieces. Following a brief silence came the chorus of "Allah akbar!"

IN THE MORNING, TALAFAR was strangely quiet except for the continuous buzzing of the unmanned Predators overhead. The Apaches were gone and the resistance was licking its wounds. It was reported that 50 mujahedeen had been killed and another 120 wounded. The worst news of all was that the Emir had been killed, the target of a Predator missile that had successfully destroyed his Land Rover. While his followers celebrated his martyrdom, the Emir's death left a power vacuum among the mujahedeen.

Around mid-morning, a group of gunmen arrived at the workshop to take us away. Zeynep pleaded with them in Turkish that we were to go free, but it was to no avail. "We received no such instruction," said the man who now appeared to be in charge. "You are spies."

This time they were extremely rough in applying my blindfold. It was tied so tight I could sense losing blood circulation in my brain. They pushed and prodded me blindly towards a car and then deliberately bashed my head against the doorframe. "Jewish pig!" spat one of the guards.

At the fourth house, which smelled like some sort of farm complex, I was once again rushed through doorways and then down into a cellar. In addition to the blindfold they placed a hood over my head and I felt I was suffocating in the heat and dust. I could feel the fear well up inside me as one of the gunmen forced me onto a mat and placed the barrel of a Kalashnikov against my neck. "Don't speak," he said. "Don't move."

Another group of men entered the cellar and began questioning Zeynep as to our identity. She told them of the Emir's promise, and advised them that our papers, ID and passports were all at the first house. Finally, we were allowed to remove the hoods while the mujahedeen went to check out our story. At this point I realized that there was another prisoner in the room with us. He was an Iraqi from Mosul, and also accused of spying. He was not allowed to remove his hood.

Throughout the rest of the morning, there was plenty of activity in the resistance bunker. About thirty or so fighters were busy transferring stockpiles of RPGs and explosives. In addition to the gruff male voices, we could hear an elderly woman shouting encouragement to the men. "They call her 'mother'," whispered Zeynep. "She is encouraging her 'sons' to go out and become martyrs and die in battle. Can you believe it?"

Our previous interrogator returned to our makeshift cell to advise us that our bags, cameras, and identity papers were now buried in a heap of rubble: The first house had been destroyed by a precision-guided bomb. With no proof of our nationality or profession, a heated debate among the fighters soon erupted outside in the corridor.

Listening to their conversation, Zeynep suddenly gasped: "Oh my god — they're going to shoot us!" I fought to suppress the panic that I felt. It was then the other prisoner spoke for the first time. In good English he said, "Are you sure?"

The door burst open and several men stepped inside. "Stand up," one of them said to me. "You are the first to die, American pig." My hands were still tied and I felt helpless as one of them approached me with another blindfold. I told them that I did not want a blindfold — not out of any bravado, but because I found that the sense of fear was magnified by the inability to see. I received a punch on the head for my protest and the blindfold was pulled snugly into place. This time they added a gag and a black hood.

Once again, I could feel the claustrophobia and fear beginning to panic me, and I struggled to maintain some composure. The cries of fear and alarm from Zeynep had caught the attention of the woman, who apparently had not realized that the men were detaining a female. She entered our cell and a heated discussion took place between her and the fighters. Several times I was struck during this conversation and I still believed I was about to die. Finally one of the mujahedeen came close to me and whispered, "I have a brother in Canada… I have just saved you my friend — at least for now."

Instead of being shot, they had decided to take us with them. They had learned that the Americans were about to bomb their complex so they were going to leave Talafar until the air strikes were over. The hood and mask remained in place, and the man who said he'd saved me warned me not to make any noise. "If my people hear someone speak English they will beat you to death before I can stop them — now move!"

Once again I was roughly manhandled through the passageways and pushed into the backseat of a car. I was shaking uncontrollably as I realized that I was not going to die — at least not that moment.

ALTHOUGH THE AMERICANS HAD CLAIMED they had "sealed off" Talafar prior to launching their offensive, I soon learned it was nothing more than wishful thinking. We had left the bunker in a six car convoy and made our way northwards into the open desert. It had taken some time before the mujahedeen in our car had relented and allowed us to remove our hoods and blindfolds. Our hands were still tied, but I had sweated so much in the 45° heat that the moisture had loosened the straps. I was able to free my hands easily and, in an effort to gain their trust, had shown them that my bonds needed to be retied. The man next to me had simply laughed and instructed them to "forget about it".... After all, where can you go in the desert?

As we began chatting, this short grey–haired man with a close–cropped beard informed me that his brother was the now–deceased Emir. "I'm sorry about his death," I said to which he replied, "Why be sorry? We celebrate his entry into Heaven."

What was reassuring to me was that, as the brother of the former leader, this man appeared to have filled the immediate leadership void in the group. I was especially relieved to learn that his brother had told him of the decision to set us free. We were also told that we had only to have our identities confirmed — via a Google search on the Internet — and he would keep the promise of the martyred Emir. In the meantime, we would remain with the mujahedeen.

AROUND 2 P.M. WE HAD STOPPED near a remote desert house. Nearly 30 fighters had assembled around our car and began to conduct a mass prayer. Zeynep and I were instructed to remain in the car. It was as they were engrossed in their prayer that I spotted the two American helicopters coming out of the south — low and fast and headed straight towards our parked convoy. I cried out in alarm. At first the mujahedeen were angry at the interruption until they too spotted the approaching threat. Caught out in the open, they were sitting ducks. Nobody could move; they simply watched the helicopters steadily bear down on us.

At about 800 metres distance, the gunships inexplicably banked away to the east without so much as a reconnaissance overpass of our mysterious group of vehicles in the middle of the desert. We had to have been in plain view, but the Americans turned away. "They always fly the same patrol routes" explained one of the fighters. "They see nothing."

Shortly after the helicopters had departed two additional cars joined us and the mujahedeen began hastily transferring the huge stockpiles of explosives and rockets into them. "We are making them into suicide bombs," said Mubashir, the Emir's brother, of the cars being loaded and wired.

"These men will head back into Talafar and use the vehicles to destroy the American armoured vehicles." A total of four mujahedeen climbed into the suicide cars and as they drove back into the battle, their comrades shouted a final encouragement.

We proceeded on through the desert towards the northern outskirts of Mosul. Along the way we stopped at several farmhouses where the residents eagerly offered the fighters food and water. When we actually entered the Mosul checkpoint, the Iraqi police appeared to take no notice of the dusty column of cars packed with bearded men armed with Kalashnikovs and RPGs. A gauntlet of young boys lined the route to cheer our convoy and offer water and cigarettes. Instead of entering the city however, we headed further north to a deserted house that was still under construction. We were ordered inside the building, and it was at this point I realized that the other hostage, a driver for UNICEF, had spent the entire 3 hour desert transit in the trunk of one of the cars. He emerged from the vehicle, still blindfolded, covered in dust and sweat, and without his shoes. He was in terrible condition, but he made no sound of complaint as they hurried us into the empty house.

There was some confusion among the fighters at this point. They were eager to return to Talafar — not sit out the battle in a safe house. All but one of their cars soon departed, leaving only two armed guards with us. The possibility of escape certainly crossed my mind. It was the hottest part of the day and the sentries were exhausted. Although it was open ground, the Mosul highway was clearly visible about 2 kilometres away. With all the passing traffic it would be possible to flag down a ride — if I could only survive the run.

Before I could give much thought to such a plan, another car pulled up at our hideout. Four new mujahedeen strode into our building and immediately began berating the two guards for being lenient with us. The leader of this group was a short, stocky, little man who strutted about with his ski-mask on. He wasted no time in making his thoughts known. "The Turkish girl will live... you two will die," he said pointing at me and the UNICEF driver. "I will cut off your heads at dusk and you will be buried there," pointing to a freshly dug grave-sized ditch about twenty metres from the house.

Zeynep was removed to another room and we were told to prepare ourselves to die. Although forbidden to talk, whenever the guard was distracted the driver and I took the opportunity to encourage each other and try to provide support. "At least we will not die alone," he said.

As dusk approached we were offered a final meal of flatbread, roast chicken and tomatoes. The maniacal little leader came to watch us eat, all the while aiming his gun at us. "Eat, eat… Why do you have no appetite? Are you afraid American pig?" he asked and then laughed at his own joke. Although I was certainly not hungry, I did my best to choke down a few difficult mouthfuls. Inside, I had to stifle a trembling fear from overcoming my composure. My fellow prisoner began to sob, and I reached over to take his hand.

"How long do you think the pain will last?" he asked. It was something which I had been giving careful consideration and I replied, "About three seconds." As the sun started to set on the horizon, Mubashir drove up and entered into a heated argument with the newcomer. Reassured at the sound of his voice, I had risked a glance out of the window just in time to see the ceremonial dagger being returned to the trunk of the car. We had been spared once again.

WHEN IT HAD PROVED IMPOSSIBLE to enter Mosul safely, we had circled back into the desert and spent the night at another farmhouse. The scorching heat of the day was replaced by a cool breeze, and after a meal of lamb and rice we had spent a relatively relaxing evening under the stars. It was the first good sleep that I'd had in days and I began to believe that with Mubashir to protect us, we would survive this ordeal.

It was during some candid conversations at this farm that I finally learned the identity of my captors. As we talked about the various ethnic factions and politics at play in northern Iraq, I had mentioned the group Ansar al-Islam. Mubashir had looked surprised at my comment and said, "Don't you know? *We* are Ansar al-Islam." My heart sank when I heard this because I knew that this group of fundamentalist extremists had links to al-Qaeda. "Yes," confided Mubashir, "Osama is our brother in Afghanistan, and al-Zaqarwi is our brother in Jordan."

This group had never before released a foreigner and this revelation explained why they had never mentioned ransoming us off as hostages.

The Ansar al-Islam fought for their religious beliefs, not money. Although I expressed my fears to Mubashir, he once again stressed the fact that his brother's wish would be granted — provided we were telling the truth.

We spent Friday morning at the farm awaiting word that we could enter Mosul and be granted an audience with the new Emir. Again, everything seemed to be relaxed, and although the notion of having someone pronounce a 'live-or-die' sentence upon me was still very frightening, Mubashir assured us that his brother's promise would be kept. We got the word around 2 p.m. that the Emir would see us. We climbed into one car — the UNICEF driver in the trunk, Zeynep and I along with Mubashir and two guards in the front. Our hands were not tied and we wore no blindfolds; everything seemed to be going well. However, once inside Mosul, it became apparent that something had gone wrong with the plan.

We had stopped at several homes and picked up different guides at various locations. Eventually we were taken to a large house in a northern suburb, and led into an empty room. The UNICEF driver was released from the trunk and taken into a small anteroom beneath a staircase. Mubashir had complained of being ill, and he now seemed disinterested in our fate. There were about a dozen young men inside this house and they were extremely hostile towards us. Blankets were placed across all the windows despite the soaring temperature.

Zeynep whispered that these new men were not Turkmen but Arabs, as she no longer understood their conversation. Mubashir made some sort of statement to them on our behalf and then bade us farewell. He and his men were heading back into Talafar to join the fight.

Within minutes of his departure, the Arabs burst into the room and roughly blindfolded me. As I tried to protest, I was kicked in the ribs, knocking the wind out of me. "Shut up American spy!" shouted my assailant.

For the next hour, I was interrogated. Again they began with their presumption that I was either a CIA or Mossad spy. I gave all the possible details of my identity and when asked how I could confirm these "lies" I told them to research my writings on the Internet. In particular, they could not believe that I had written features for al-Jazeera's website. Although intense, I was relieved when the questioning had ended without any physical force being used. I was premature in my assumption.

I had barely removed the blindfold and taken a sip of water when five men rushed back into the room. I could see the batons and ropes, but I had no time to react before I was pulled to my feet. When I attempted to resist, my feet were knocked out from under me, and I was savagely kicked. They blindfolded me and gagged me with a headscarf. My hands were tied behind my back and I was rolled over with my feet up in the air and tied to a pole. Two men held the pole up as two others beat my feet with straps and batons.

At first I could not see the blows coming but then one of my attackers, in his pent up fury, struck my face several times with his fist and knocked my blindfold aside slightly so that I could see from the corner of my eye. I mentally promised myself not to give them the satisfaction of hearing me scream until after the 20th blow. I bit down hard on the cloth and focussed on counting rather than the pain. I kept my promise, and on the 21st strike I screamed out "Fuck!," the cloth muffling the sound somewhat. With each successive blow I uttered the same expletive. Deliberately, they repeatedly hit the same spot on my thigh. For the first four or five blows the pain would increase incrementally and then the next strike would force an involuntary convulsion. I could feel the pain explode in my head and my body jackknifed upwards reflexively.

In these instances I found myself blurting out "Jeeesus Christ!" through my gritted teeth. I lost all track of time — I could have been tortured for 5 minutes or 25 — I have no real conception of the actual duration. I do remember that despite the excruciating pain in my legs, I kept fearing that the next blow would be to my genitals. With my legs splayed apart and upended I felt incredibly vulnerable. When the beating finally stopped, I felt a tremendous sense of relief that they had not used the batons on my crotch.

After my feet were cut loose, I was roughly pulled upright and the interrogator handed me a pen and paper. "You will write down all the websites you think might help to confirm that you are in fact a Canadian journalist," he said. I made some remark that I would have gladly done so without the beating, but my attempt at black humour was wasted.

I had been badly beaten and as I walked out of the anteroom back into the main parlour, most of the Arab 'pupils' had gathered to see my reaction. I tried my best not to let them see any weakness by pressing the pen hard against the paper so that they could not see my hands shaking. Taking the list of websites from me, the interrogator told me, "If this checks out, you'll live... If you lied — you die."

A few minutes later, I was ushered into an adjacent room, told to lie face down on the floor and a gun barrel was placed against the back of my neck. It was Zeynep's turn to be beaten, and as she cried out in pain, the guard behind me kept repeating, "You can spare her the pain — simply confess that you are a spy." I continued to utter denials, so he spat on my head and said, "Only a dog would let a woman suffer like that!" I thought to myself, "And what kind of animal would torture a woman?"

For several hours after the beating, I was kept alone in that room. My legs were aching and would occasionally seize up on me. I tried to stand, but the guards insisted that I remain seated on a mat. When the interrogator finally re-entered my holding cell he said, "You failed the test on the Internet. Prepare yourself to die — tonight." As the door banged shut behind him, I once again had an all-consuming sense of dread. The next time the door opened it was an armed guard and one of the 'pupils' carrying a platter of food. Once again I was being encouraged to eat my final meal.

I did not know it at the time, Zeynep and the UNICEF driver had been set free, while both of them were told that I had been beheaded.

After I picked away at my food, the dishes were cleared away and a heavy set young Arab entered the room. He was grinning from ear to ear and I recognized him as one of my torturers. "I am the lucky one who has been chosen to kill you, American dog," he said.

It was at this time I decided to play my final card. Zeynep had always told me that I should tell our captors I wished to convert to Islam — even if I wasn't sincere, she thought it might buy me time (if not freedom). "I want you to teach me an Islamic prayer before you kill me." I said, "A man about to die should have a God to pray to, shouldn't he?" Other guards and pupils had overheard this and they seemed excited at the prospect of converting a 'Kaffir' and then executing him.

As they started to explain the conversion process and necessary prayers, one of the clerics returned to the house. He put an end to the commotion by informing me my religious conversion was no longer necessary as I was "free to go." Thinking this may be yet another test of my resolve to convert, I explained that in that case it was even more important, "as a man needs a God to thank for sparing him his life."

I was advised that the procedure would have to be performed at a later date, as a car was waiting to take me to a safe house in preparation for my release. Once again, I dared to start believing that I might actually survive this ordeal.

MY EYES WERE TAPED SHUT with electrical tape and my sunglasses placed on top. I was then led gently to a car outside. The night air felt cool and refreshing and I tried to keep my euphoria in check, reminding myself that it was not over yet.

However, by the time we had driven several kilometres and my escorts led me inside a new house, I felt certain that I had been saved. The glasses were taken off and the tape removed. I found myself in a clean home sitting on a bed looking at three smiling Arabs. My guards from the other house were in the doorway and one of them waved his hand in a fluttering motion, smiled and said, "Free…. Bye, bye." The door shut behind them and all of a sudden the three Arabs stopped smiling. The big man standing in the centre of the room strode towards me pulling a pair of handcuffs from behind his back. The nightmare started all over.

THEY CUFFED MY HANDS behind my back and instructed me to sleep. Two of them slept in the same room as me — armed with pistols — while the home owner had taken the precaution of padlocking us in. It proved impossible to sleep with my arms pinned back like that and after two hours I felt stabbing pain in my shoulders. In an attempt to alleviate the pressure, I tried to sit up on the edge of the bed. Startled by my movement, one of the Arabs put his pistol to my forehead and motioned for me to lie back down. For the next six hours I could do nothing but try to block out the pain.

The following morning it became clear that instead of taking me to a safe house en route to freedom, I had been transferred to yet another fundamentalist faction. At about 10 a.m. I was 'prepped' for my new interrogation by having my feet and hands chained to the bed and my eyes once again taped firmly shut. I estimated that at least three additional terrorists entered the room and began talking with my guards. Anticipating yet another beating, I fought to control my fear. One man simply stated in excellent English, "We know that you are a Mossad spy." As I started to protest he interrupted me, "Don't waste your breath. You have 24 hours to decide whether to tell the truth and die with a clear conscience… or go to your death as a liar. That is your choice. Think it over." With that said, the newcomers promptly left the house.

I spent that entire day chained to the bed and for the most part blindfolded. As a gesture of compassion they would occasionally free my eyes so that I could watch the television. All the programming was focused on the anniversary of the World Trade Center attacks. It was September 11th, and I was tied to a bed in an al-Qaeda cell house in Iraq. I felt my fate was truly sealed.

With so many hours to once again contemplate my own death I began to think of all the practical aspects that would be attendant upon my demise. My family would have been informed of my capture and death by Zeynep Tugrul — if indeed she had been released — so my thoughts drifted to things such as, How would they repatriate the body? Was there a process for moving corpses out of Iraq? Who would take care of the funeral arrangements? etc.

That evening I was once again asked what I would prefer as my "final meal." After arguing, again, that my appetite wasn't exactly stimulated by my imminent death, I asked for roast chicken. When the food arrived, they kept one of my hands tied to the bed and a pistol aimed at the back of my head. It seemed they were taking no chances in letting me escape execution.

It was only 9 p.m. — just 11 hours after they first came, not the promised 24 — when the three other terrorists returned. I did not feel cheated out of the time, as I was actually dreading the thought of another night of agony in the handcuffs. I had made my peace with God and if necessary, I was prepared to die. Another 13 hours of mental anguish was not necessary.

As soon as everyone was settled around my bed, the interrogator said that I did not have to fear any torture as this round of questioning would be far more straightforward. "It is either life or knife, with each answer that you give us," he said, "So please relax." For over one hour I carefully answered all their questions — careful to avoid the obvious traps. For instance, when asked, "Have you ever visited the State of Israel?" I answered,

"No, I have never been to the occupied State of Palestine."

I have no idea whether or not my answers were convincing — in fact, I suspect that the decision to release me had already been made at some higher level — but during what would be the last of my lengthy replies, the interrogator suddenly said, "Stop. Get your things. You will live. You are free."

Once the handcuffs were removed, I was handed my shoes and jacket and it seemed as though they were the ones anxious to be rid of me. Still with my eyes taped shut, I was driven to a highway where one of the guards flagged down a passing taxi. Another man ripped the tape off my eyes, pushed 10,000 dinars ($6 U.S.) into my shirt pocket and pushed me head first into the back of the cab.

I was free.

Author Scott Taylor was photographed outside the Iraqi Turkmen Front office in Ankara, Turkey, after his release.